A Parent's Guide to the Common Core

Grade 3

© 2014 Kaplan, Inc.

Published by Kaplan Publishing, a division of Kaplan, Inc.
395 Hudson Street
New York, NY 10014

Printed in the United States of America

10 9 8 7 6 5 4 3 2 1

ISBN-13: 978-1-61865-822-7

Kaplan Publishing books are available at special quantity discounts to use for sales promotions, employee premiums, or educational purposes. For more information or to purchase books, please call the Simon & Schuster special sales department at 866-506-1949.

A PARENT'S GUIDE TO THE COMMON CORE: GRADE **3**

TABLE OF CONTENTS

This book is designed to introduce you and your child to the Common Core Standards, a major development in the way U.S. students are taught the most basic and critical areas of knowledge that they will encounter while in school. The Common Core Standards will be used to create assessments beginning in the 2014-2015 school year.

Where did the Common Core Standards come from?

The Common Core Standards were developed to create more uniform academic standards across the United States. Since each state has traditionally created its own academic standards and assessments, students in one state would often end up studying different things than students in another state. Education professionals from across the nation worked together to select the best and most relevant standards from all the states, and then used these as the basis for new standards that could be used by every state to ensure that all students are fully prepared for the future. The Common Core Standards are, in many cases, more comprehensive and demanding than previous state standards. These new standards are designed to help American students perform favorably against students from other developed nations—an area in which the United States has fallen behind in recent years.

The Common Core Standards were not created by the federal government. Each state may choose whether it wishes to use the Common Core Standards, or stick with its own unique learning standards. However, most states have recognized the importance of consistent and high-level standards for all American students. At printing, forty-five states, along with the District of Columbia and four U.S. territories, have adopted the Common Core Standards.

What are the Common Core Standards?

The Common Core Standards are the standards to which all students will be held. These standards are applicable for grades K-12. The Common Core Standards focus on two areas of learning: English Language Arts and Mathematics. These areas were chosen because they are critical to developing a solid foundation for learning, and encompass other fields such as social studies and science.

Within English Language Arts, the Common Core Standards are divided into several categories: Reading; Writing; Speaking & Listening; and Language. For Grade 3, reading standards are focused on basic understanding of reading passages, and identifying how specific details and ideas are expressed within the text. Writing standards focus on basic structure, including event sequencing and creating writing with opening and concluding statements. Students will also be asked to write opinion pieces in which they use evidence to support their views. These skills are critical for building a foundation for success, both in school and in later life.

Within Mathematics, the Common Core Standards are also divided into several categories. For Grade 3, these categories are: Operations & Algebraic Thinking; Number & Operations in Base Ten; Number & Operations—Fractions; Measurement & Data; and Geometry. For Grade 3, Operations & Algebraic Thinking focuses mainly on understanding the principles of basic multiplication and division. Number & Operations—Fractions focuses on the basic properties of fractions. Measurement & Data focuses on measuring the area of rectangles, as well as measuring and estimating volumes and mass. These skills have been identified as critical for success in other areas such as the sciences.

The Common Core Standards do not dictate a teacher's curriculum; they just ensure that all teachers are working toward the same learning standards. Teachers were instrumental in developing the standards, and remain the dominant force in helping your child achieve academic potential. However, as a parent, you now have the opportunity to see the "road map" that your child's teachers will be using to build their courses of study. This allows you to better become an active participant in helping your child achieve these learning goals.

How to Use this Book

This book is designed to provide you with the tools necessary to help your child succeed. While the Common Core Standards are numerous for each grade level, Kaplan's learning experts have identified the standards that are most critical for success, both in the classroom and on assessment tests. These are known as the "power standards." Each lesson in this book is dedicated to a different power standard. The power standards are also the focus of the tests and quizzes throughout the book.

You should begin by having your child take the Pre-Test for each domain. The Pre-Test is designed to cover the same skills that will likely be tested on state assessments. This will give you an idea of the areas in which your child excels, as well as the areas that may need special attention.

Once you have gauged your child's baseline skills, the lessons offer practical experience with each of the power standards. Each lesson provides information on what the standard means, and offers examples of how the standard might be addressed through classroom teaching and through testing. In addition, each lesson offers an activity that you can engage in with your child to help practice the skills highlighted in the lesson. Once you are confident in your child's abilities with regard to a lesson, you can have your child take the end-of-lesson quiz for that power standard to ensure mastery.

When you have completed all the lessons, have your child complete the Post-Test for each domain. You can compare your child's performance on the Post-Test to the Pre-Test, and see which areas have improved the most. If some areas still need work, re-read the corresponding lesson with your child, and try to pinpoint the specific issue that your child needs additional help mastering. The List of Resources provided with this book includes a number of Web sites, publications, and other types of resources that can help you and your child continue to practice and reinforce the Common Core Standards.

Common Core State Standards Initiative http://www.corestandards.org/.
This Web site offers in-depth information about the Common Core Standards and their history.

National Library of Virtual Manipulatives http://nlvm.usu.edu/en/nav/vlibrary.html.
This National Science Foundation supported project allows students, teachers, and parents to interact with virtual manipulatives that can aid in teaching basic mathematic principles.

Learning Resources Shop: Math Manipulatives http://www.learningresources.com/category/teachers /shop+by+category/manipulatives/math.do.
This educational supplier offers a variety of manipulatives that can be used by you and your child to master basic math concepts.

Math Videos by Math Playground http://www.mathplayground.com/mathvideos.html.
These videos address a wide range of math-related questions, from "How do you add fractions?" to "How do you solve an inequality?"

New Common Core Math Problems and Resources https://www.khanacademy.org/commoncore.
Khan Academy, one of the world's premier not-for-profit online classrooms, offers practice problems that are mapped to the specific Common Core Standards and organized by grade level.

Free Activities and Worksheets from Flashkids http://www.flashkids.com/free-downloads.
These activities and worksheets are broken down by domain and grade level, and can be a fun way to improve skills critical to Common Core.

Parents' Guide to Student Success, 3rd Grade http://pta.org/files//3rd%20Grade_B-W.pdf.
This overview from the National Parent-Teacher Association tells you in detail what you should expect from a curriculum aimed at meeting Common Core Standards.

Parent Roadmaps to the Common Core Standards—English Language Arts http://www.cgcs.org /Domain/36.
The Council of the Great City Schools offers parent roadmaps to help you support your child in math and English language arts at each grade level.

Working with the "Shifts" http://www.engageny.org/sites/default/files/resource/attachments/parent _workshop_what_parents_can_do_handout.pdf.
This handout from the New York State Education Department explains in detail how the Common Core

Standards have shifted the content and methods used by teachers, and offers suggestions for how you can help your student thrive amid these changes.

Achieve the Core http://www.achievethecore.org/.
This Web site was created by the main creators of the Common Core Standards as a way to provide free teaching materials tailored to help students master the skills needed to meet these standards.

PBS Parents: Reading & Language http://www.pbs.org/parents/education/reading-language/.
This Web site, affiliated with the Public Broadcasting Service (PBS), offers advice for improving your child's literacy and love of reading.

ReadWriteThink Tips & How-To Resources for Parents http://www.readwritethink.org/search/?grade=8-12&resource_type=74.
This site, supported by the International Reading Association and the National Council of Teachers of English, provides tips to help parents nurture their child's interest in reading and the language arts.

Black Beauty **by Anna Sewell**
This novel, available in the public domain, is an excellent text for third-grade readers. It offers vivid descriptions of life from the point of view of a horse.

American Library Association Summer Reading List, Grades 3-5 http://www.ala.org/alsc/sites/ala.org.alsc/files/content/SummerReadingList_3-5_BW.pdf.
This list, aimed at keeping kids involved in reading during their summer months, includes titles that are highly recommended by student readers at the same grade level as your child.

ENGLISH LANGUAGE ARTS PRE-TEST

The pre-test is intended as a preliminary assessment of your child's language arts skills. The questions cover reading comprehension, vocabulary, and writing. There are a variety of question types at various levels of cognition. These are typical of the types of questions that your third grader might experience in the classroom, as homework, and in assessment situations.

A grid at the end provides the main Common Core standard assessed, as well as a brief explanation of the correct answers. This is intended to provide information about which standards your child might need the most help with. Because of this, encourage your child to take an educated guess on questions that he or she is unsure of, but also ask him or her to put a star or question mark next to it. This will help you identify areas that might need some reinforcement.

The items on the pre-test are **not** designed to replicate standardized tests used to assess a child's reading level or a school's progress in helping the child achieve grade level.

Read the following two paragraphs aloud to your child:

> This test includes questions to test reading and writing skills. Please answer as best as possible. The test will not be graded. If you come across a question that you are unsure of, put a question mark next to it and make your best guess.

> Some of the questions are based on stories or other reading passages. Read the passage carefully. If you don't know the answer to a question, look back at the passage to see if you can find it.

> **Directions:** For each section, read the passage and then answer the questions that follow.

 ### Aunt Ria's Dolls

Going to Aunt Ria's house was so much fun! Aunt Ria was an airline pilot and had traveled to many different countries. Her house was like a museum. Shelves lined the room showing off knick-knacks from all corners of the world.

My favorite of Aunt Ria's treasures was a stackable doll from Russia. It looked just like one doll on the outside. When you opened the doll, it would reveal a slightly smaller doll inside. This smaller doll also could be opened to reveal yet another doll. They went on and on until you reached a tiny doll at the center.

"Can I look at the dolls?" I called in to the kitchen. Aunt Ria was making dinner.

"Of course, Mara," replied Aunt Ria. "Just be careful!"

As Aunt Ria went to make dinner, I played with the dolls. I examined the red doll, wondering how the artist was able to paint her so perfectly. Then I twisted it carefully. Sure enough, the next doll wore a bright dress of orange. I took my time opening each doll, trying to imagine what it would be like to paint them. I pretended that they were a family, lined up ready to march off to school. I got to the pink doll. Already small, I twisted her open in anticipation of the final doll. I gasped! The final doll was missing!

My first thought was to cover up the crime. The tiny purple doll had always been my favorite. Last time I had visited Aunt Ria, I had taken it to the guestroom. Had I forgotten to put it back?

I quickly put the dolls back together, hoping to find the doll before Aunt Ria noticed it was missing. Pink into blue, blue into green, into yellow, into orange, and red . . . back on the shelf they went. Then, I flew off into the guestroom to see if I could find the tiniest doll of all.

I looked everywhere I could think of, but I couldn't find the doll. By the time Aunt Ria called me for dinner, my guilt weighed me down like a hundred-pound weight. I skulked into the kitchen.

"The dolls were beautiful as usual," I said. I swallowed the lump in my throat and continued. "I especially love that little doll. You know, the purple one on the very inside?"

"Do you mean this one?" Aunt Ria said, holding out the little doll in her hand.

"Yes." I was surprised to see the tiny doll in Aunt Ria's hand.

"Why did you tell me you just saw it?"

"I didn't want you to be mad that I had lost it," I said quietly.

"Sweetheart, lying is never the answer. I found it in the guestroom when I was getting it ready for you, but I couldn't remember which doll it went to. Is that what you were doing in the guestroom all this time? Looking for the doll?"

"Yes. I'm sorry I lost it!"

"Don't be silly. It wasn't lost. It was being loved. Everyone deserves to be loved, even the tiniest dolls like this one."

The doll was even tinier than I remembered. I marveled at the tiny features, the perfect red of a mouth and eyes no bigger than pinpricks. "It's beautiful."

"Yes, it's perfect," said Aunt Ria with a smile. "Just like my niece."

❓ Questions

1. Read the sentence from the passage. "My first thought was to cover up the crime." What is this crime?

   A. *losing the doll*

   B. *breaking the doll*

   C. *lying about the doll*

   D. *playing with the doll*

2. Read the sentence from the passage. "I swallowed the lump in my throat." Why did Mara have a lump in her throat?

   A. *She was eating.*

   B. *She felt happy.*

   C. *She was hungry.*

   D. *She felt nervous.*

3. Which best describes the main message of the passage?

   A. *Things are easily lost.*

   B. *You should not lie about problems.*

   C. *Things that are lost are easily found.*

   D. *You should not play with beautiful things.*

4. Why does Mara say Aunt Ria's house is like a museum?

    A. *There are dolls from Russia.*

    B. *There are museums in many places.*

    C. *There are rules about touching things.*

    D. *There are things from all over the world.*

5. Use your own words to write a paragraph describing Aunt Ria. Do you think she is kind? Explain your answer. Use details from the story. Use correct grammar, punctuation, and spelling.

    _____

    _____

    _____

    _____

 ## Uh Oh!

Will woke to the sound of chirping just outside his window. He stretched his arms over his head and wiggled his toes. He rubbed his eyes in an attempt to erase the night's effect.

Will swung his legs out from under the blankets and stepped out onto the cool floor. He opened the blinds to see a bright, sunny day. He watched a squirrel nibble on an acorn and then hop toward the driveway. It was then that he noticed Mr. Green's car in the street.

"Uh oh!" said Will. Mr. Green only parked in the street on Saturdays, and Will had an early soccer game. He looked at his alarm clock. It was 7:55 and his game was scheduled for 8:00! He raced out his door and almost ran into his dad.

The words rushed from Will's mouth. "Dad! Soccer!"

"Calm down, Will," his dad said calmly. "The coach called last night to say all the games today are going to start an hour later than usual. Go ahead and get ready. We'll grab a bite to eat on the way to the game."

Questions

6. Why is Will upset?

    A. *He thinks he overslept.*

    B. *The birds woke him up.*

    C. *He does not want to play soccer.*

    D. *He will not have time for breakfast.*

7. Read the following sentence from the story: "He rubbed his eyes in an attempt to erase the night's effect." What is happening in this sentence?

    A. *He had a nightmare.*

    B. *He is trying to wake up.*

    C. *He is trying to see in the dark.*

    D. *He wants to get rid of pencil marks.*

8. What misunderstanding is central to the story?

    A. *It is not Saturday.*

    B. *The car is not Mr. Green's.*

    C. *Will's soccer game is not at 8:00.*

    D. *Will does not have a soccer game today.*

 ## A Race to the Moon

On May 25, 1961, President John F. Kennedy made a speech. He told people that he wanted the United States to land on the moon by the end of the decade.

Kennedy's idea sounded crazy to many people. It was only one month after a Russian named Yuri Gagarin had become the first person in space. It was only 20 days after Alan Shepard had become the first American in space. These men had been in rocket-like satellites that splashed down in the ocean. Landing on the moon was very different.

Kennedy's ideas did not sound crazy to some of the scientists at NASA. In 1963 they started the Apollo program. The main goal of the Apollo program was to get a team of astronauts to the moon.

The scientists started by sending unmanned satellites into space. These test flights allowed the scientists to test the systems without putting people in danger. It took a long time to build the satellites and improve all the systems. The first Apollo spacecraft that had people on board was sent into space in October 1968. This was Apollo 7. In December 1968, Apollo 8 became the first to orbit the moon. Apollo 9 was launched in March 1969 and Apollo 10 in May.

It was with Apollo 11 that American scientists and astronauts achieved Kennedy's goal. Apollo 11 included the "Eagle," which was a small vehicle that would allow the astronauts to land on the moon. On July 20, 1969, astronauts Neil Armstrong and Edward "Buzz" Aldrin piloted the Eagle to the moon. The third astronaut, Michael Collins, stayed on the Apollo spacecraft as it orbited the moon. Armstrong stepped down a ladder onto the surface of the moon. As he stepped on the last step of the ladder, he said, "That's one small step for man; one giant leap for mankind."

Questions

9. Look at the events from the story. Then, put them in the order that they happened.

    ___ *The Apollo program begins.*

    ___ *The first man steps onto the moon.*

    ___ *The first manned spacecraft is launched.*

    ___ *President Kennedy says he wants to reach the moon.*

10. Why did the scientists send unmanned satellites into space before Apollo 11? Answer using complete sentences.

    _____

    _____

11. Match the following people to their accomplishments:

    Neil Armstrong   *first man in space*

    Yuri Gagarin   *first American in space*

    Alan Shepard   *first man on the moon*

12. How did most Americans feel about Kennedy's decision to put a man on the moon? Why? Answer using complete sentences.

_____

_____

_____

13. Write a paragraph telling the story of Apollo 11 and why it was important. Use details from the passage. Make sure to use correct grammar, punctuation, and spelling.

_____

_____

_____

_____

_____

_____

 The Twin Towers

Lauren and Julia are twins. They are the tallest girls in their class and the best players on the basketball team. It was their coach who first dubbed them the "twin towers." The name caught on, and soon everyone would talk about Lauren and Julia by this nickname. Lauren and Julia liked the name because it made them feel special.

Lauren and Julia were a lot alike. They both loved basketball and swimming. They had many of the same friends.

But Lauren and Julia were also different. Lauren laughed louder than Julia. She was always the first to answer a question when it was asked of the two of them. And while they both loved movies, Lauren preferred funny movies while Julia liked dramas. Julia especially loved dogs—dog movies were her favorite.

Julia thought that Lauren had nicer clothes than she did. Lauren did not like to share her things. Lauren sometimes borrowed Julia's clothes, but Lauren rarely let Julia borrow anything from her. When Julia lost her goggles, Lauren would not let her borrow any even though she had an extra pair.

Questions

14. Read the following sentence from the passage: "It was their coach who first dubbed them the 'twin towers.'" Based on context clues, what does "dub" mean?

_____

_____

15. Why did the coach call Lauren and Julia the "twin towers"?

_____

_____

16. Read the last paragraph. Based on this paragraph, how would you describe Lauren? Give a detail from the paragraph to support your answer.

_____

_____

17. Write a paragraph comparing Lauren and Julia. How are they alike? How are they different? Use your own words to write your paragraph. Make sure your paragraph is free of errors.

_____

_____

_____

_____

 Art of Africa

There are many different kinds of African art. Some parts of Africa are known for brightly colored cloth. One type of cloth, called *kente,* is woven from silk and cotton. Africa also has a long history of making jewelry from metal, shells, ivory, and gems. Long ago, the people of Africa also made sculptures of people and animals from terracotta, a type of clay. People of Africa have also made masks for many years.

Not all African masks are the same. People made the masks from the materials they had available. Some African masks are made of wood with eyes carved out. Others are painted. Some masks are decorated with shells, colored beads, hair pieces, or other materials. Other masks are painted or carved with bold patterns and shapes.

Questions

18. Which sentence from the passage tells the main idea?

_____

_____

19. Which could you use to make a sculpture like those of Africa?
    A. clay   C. cotton
    B. colored pencils   D. special pens

20. Why did the author write "Art in Africa"?
    A. to get people to buy African art
    B. to explain why Africans created art
    C. to show that African art is beautiful
    D. to tell about different types of African art

Read the sentences below. Then answer the questions that follow.

Sofia opened the tiny box. When she saw a twinkle of silver a smile crept across Sofia's face. She pushed aside the tissue paper to reveal the very charm she had wanted.

Questions

21. Which best describes how Sofia feels?
    A. disappointed
    B. happy
    C. lucky
    D. surprised

22. Which words best show what Sofia is feeling?
    A. the tiny box
    B. a twinkle of silver
    C. a smile crept
    D. pushed aside

23. Read the following sentences: *We wanted to go to the beach. It was raining.* Which sentence correctly connects these two ideas?
    A. We wanted to go to the beach, and it was raining.
    B. We wanted to go to the beach, but it was raining.
    C. We wanted to go to the beach, or it was raining.
    D. We wanted to go to the beach, so it was raining.

24. The following sentence has one or more errors: *Richie, and Marco went to dinner at joe's pizzeria.* Rewrite the sentence so it is correct.

    _____

    _____

25. Read this draft from a story.

    I was babysitting for Joey and Jeanna when the storm came. The lights went out. Joey and Jeanna got scared. I was scared too. I didn't want them to know I was scared. I thought that they might become even more scared if they knew how scared I was. So I got out the flashlight and made a game of it. Soon, we all forgot to be scared.

    The word *scared* has been overused in these sentences. Revise the sentences to replace *scared* with an alternative in at least two places. Underline the changes you have made.

✓ Answer Key

Note: The answers to open-ended, constructed response questions are sample answers. Answers will vary, but look for the main ideas to be included.

Highlight any questions that your child gets wrong. Looking at the wrong answers may help to reveal one or more standards with which your child is struggling. Even if your child has done well on this pre-test, reviewing the lessons will help him or her become a better reader and writer.

Passage	Question	Answer	Standard(s)
Aunt Ria's Dolls	1	A	RL.3.1
	2	D	RL.3.1, RL.3.4
	3	B	RL.3.2
	4	D	RL.3.1
	5	Aunt Ria is kind. She asks Mara to be careful with the doll, but she is not upset when Mara misplaces one of the dolls. She also reminds Mara that it is important to be honest, but she does this kindly. She even tells Mara that she is perfect!	RL.3.3; W.3.2
Uh Oh!	6	A	RL.3.1, RL.3.3
	7	B	RL.3.4
	8	C	RL.3.2
A Race to the Moon	9	(1) The first manned spacecraft is launched. (2) President Kennedy says he wants to reach the moon. (3) The Apollo program begins. (4) The first man steps onto the moon.	RI.3.3
	10	To test the systems so the rocket would be safe	RI.3.1, RI.3.2
	11	Neil Armstrong—first man on the moon; Yuri Gagarin—first man in space; Alan Shepard—first American in space	RI.3.1
	12	They were surprised. They didn't think it could be done.	RI.3.2
	13	Apollo 11 was part of the NASA space program. It carried three astronauts into space. Two of the astronauts, Neil Armstrong and Buzz Aldrin, became the first men on the moon. This was a big success. Many people did not think it could be done.	RI.3.2, W.3.2
The Twin Towers	14	named or called someone or something	RL.3.4
	15	They were tall (like towers), and they were twins.	RL.3.4
	16	Lauren is kind of selfish. She didn't like to share her clothes or her goggles with Julia.	RL.3.3
	17	Lauren and Julia are twins. They are both tall and good basketball players. They also both love swimming and watching movies. Lauren laughs louder and is more outgoing. Lauren and Julia also enjoy different kinds of movies. Julia is a bit shyer than Lauren and seems to be more generous. She allows Lauren to borrow her clothes, but Lauren does not like to share.	RL.3.3, W.3.2
Art of Africa	18	There are many different kinds of African art.	RI.3.2
	19	A	RI.3.1, RI.3.4
	20	D	RI.3.2

Passage	Question	Answer	Standard(s)
	21	B	RL.3.3
	22	C	RL.3.1
	23	B	W.3.2.c
	24	Richie and Marco went to dinner at Joe's Pizzeria.	W.3.5
	25	Answers will vary. Correct answers may replace "scared" with frightened, afraid, fearful, or another synonym. Possible answer: "I was babysitting for Joey and Jeanna when the storm came. The lights went out. Joey and Jeanna got scared. I was frightered too. I didn't want them to know how I felt. I thought that they might become even more afraid if they knew how scared I was. So I got out the flashlight and made a game of it. Soon, we all forgot to be afraid.	W.3.5

MATHEMATICS PRE-TEST

This test covers some of the most important math skills for 3rd grade. If you do not know how to answer a question, try your best. The test will not be graded. If you come across a question that you are unsure of, put a question mark next to it and make your best guess.

Quiz

1. Use the bar models to compare the fractions $\frac{2}{3}$ and $\frac{1}{3}$ and determine which one of the following statements is true.

   A. $\frac{1}{3} = \frac{2}{3}$ B. $\frac{1}{3} > \frac{2}{3}$ C. $\frac{1}{3} < \frac{2}{3}$ D. The fractions cannot be compared.

2. Sandra has made 4 gift baskets for her aunts. If each gift basket has 6 fruits, then how many fruits are in all of the gift baskets? Draw a picture and write an equation to show your work.

3. Draw the fractions $\frac{3}{4}$ and $\frac{2}{4}$ on the number lines below. Then, fill in the blank with <, >, or = to compare them.

0   1

0   1

$\frac{3}{4}$ _____ $\frac{2}{4}$

4. Which expression could be used to find the area of the figure below?

    A. $(3 \times 3) + (3 \times 2)$
    B. $(3 \times 1) + (3 \times 2)$
    C. $(3 + 3) \times (3 + 2)$
    D. $(3 + 1) \times (3 + 2)$

5. The image below represents the top of a computer desk. What is the area of the top of the computer desk?

2 feet

_____ square feet

5 feet

6. Which equation represents the situation?

"Vanessa baked some cookies and shared them with her friend Bryana. Vanessa and Bryanna each had 4 cookies. How many cookies did Vanessa bake?"

  A. $? \div 2 = 4$ B. $4 \times 2 = ?$ C. $? \times 2 = 4$ D. $4 \div 2 = ?$

7. Write a fraction that is equivalent to the fraction shown on the bar model.

Answer: _____

8. Darryl had 14 pencils and then gave 2 to his brother. The next day, he gave an equal number of pencils to each of 3 friends. How many pencils did he give to each friend?

9. The directions for a bookshelf say that it can hold up to 60 kilograms without breaking. Camilla wants to put items with a mass of 28 kilograms on the bottom shelf, 14 kilograms on the second shelf, 6,000 grams on the third shelf, and 8,000 grams on the top shelf. Can the bookshelf hold this much mass without breaking? Explain how you know.

10. What number in place of the ♥ makes the number sentence 15 ÷ ♥ = 5 true?

    Answer: _____

11. If 28 ÷ a = 7, then what is a?

    A. 21   B. 14   C. 4   D. 2

12. Mrs. Jarvic's class was collecting money in a jar so that they could donate it to a food bank. On Monday, three students each added $2.00 to the jar and on Tuesday, two students each added $4.00 to the jar. How much money did the five students add to the jar?

13. Write <, > or = to make the statement true: $\dfrac{5}{8}$ _____ $\dfrac{5}{6}$

14. Which of the following can be answered by finding 18÷2?

    A. Mark has 18 peanuts left and will divide them evenly between himself and his friend. How many peanuts will each person get?
    B. A shirt costs $18.00. How much will it cost to buy two of these shirts?
    C. Blake started the week with 18 pairs of clean socks. Now 2 of the pairs are dirty. How many clean pairs of socks are left?
    D. There are 18 people at a party when 2 more people arrive. How many people are now at the party?

15. Which number sentence is represented by the image below?

    ```
    *  *  *  *  *  *  *
    *  *  *  *  *  *  *
    ```
    A. 2 + 7 = 9
    B. 2 × 7 = 14
    C. 7 − 2 = 5
    D. 14 × 2 = 28

16. Which fraction is equivalent to $\dfrac{2}{4}$?

    A. $\dfrac{3}{6}$ B. $\dfrac{1}{4}$ C. $\dfrac{2}{6}$ D. $\dfrac{2}{2}$

17. What is the area of the figure below?

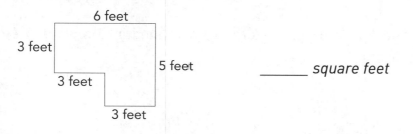

    _____ square feet

18. Which fraction is greater than 1?

    A. $\dfrac{3}{4}$ B. $\dfrac{6}{8}$ C. $\dfrac{4}{4}$ D. $\dfrac{10}{8}$

19. Mei-Yin drew the array below to show the number of rows and columns of canned goods she could store in her pantry.

    How many canned goods can Mei-Yin store in her pantry?
    A. 28   B. 32   C. 36   D. 40

20. Raul is training to run a race. He ran a total of 75 miles in three months. In the first month he ran 25 miles and in the second month he ran 30 miles. How many miles did he run in the third month?
    A. 20   B. 55   C. 100   D. 105

21. The figure below shows the layout of a bedroom and each square represents one square foot. What is the area of the room that is covered by the bed?

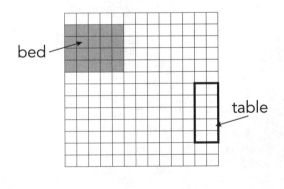

    A. 10 square feet   C. 16 square feet
    B. 13 square feet   D. 20 square feet

22. Which of the following is equivalent to the fraction $\dfrac{8}{4}$?

    A. 1   B. 2   C. 4   D. 8

23. The green peppers at a grocery store are arranged in 8 rows and 6 columns. How many green peppers are there?
    A. 14   B. 12   C. 42   D. 48

24. Which of the following items weighs about 1 kilogram?

   A. A penny   C. A big school book

   B. A big dog   D. An egg

25. Which of the following is equivalent to the fraction shown on the number line below?

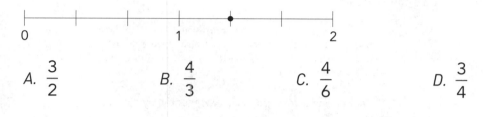

  A. $\dfrac{3}{2}$ B. $\dfrac{4}{3}$ C. $\dfrac{4}{6}$ D. $\dfrac{3}{4}$

 **Answer Key**

Question	Answer	Explanation	Standard
1	C	The bar models show that $\frac{2}{3}$ makes a greater portion of the whole than $\frac{1}{3}$.	3.NF.A.3d
2	$4 \times 6 = 24$	⊕ ⊕ ⊕ ⊕	3.OA.A.1, 3.OA.A.3
3	>	*(number lines showing $\frac{3}{4}$ and $\frac{2}{4}$)*	3.NF.A.3d
4	B	The shaded region has an area of 3×1 units while the remainder has an area of 3×2 units. Adding them will find the area of the entire region.	3.MD.C.7c
5	10 sq ft	$2 \times 5 = 10$	3.MD.C.7b
6	A	Dividing the unknown number of baked cookies evenly between two friends resulted in 4 cookies each, so ? $\div$ 2 = 4.	3.OA.A.3
7	Sample answer: $\frac{1}{2}$	The bar is divided into 4 pieces, 2 of which are shaded. This means half, or $\frac{1}{2}$ of the bar is shaded. Other possible answers are $\frac{3}{6}$ or $\frac{4}{8}$.	3.NF.A.3a, 3.NF.A.3b
8	4	$14 - 2 = 12$ and $12 \div 3 = 4$	3.OA.D.8
9	Yes	1,000 grams = 1 kilogram, so 6,000 grams = 6 kilograms and 8,000 grams = 8 kilograms. $28 + 14 + 6 + 8 = 56$ and $56 < 60$.	3.MD.A.2

Question	Answer	Explanation	Standard
10	3	$15 \div 3 = 5$	3.OA.A.4
11	C	$28 \div 4 = 7$	3.OA.A.4
12	$14	$3 \times 2 + 2 \times 4 = 6 + 8 = 14$	3.OA.D.8
13	$\frac{5}{8} < \frac{5}{6}$	The fractions have the same numerator, so they have the same number of parts. The fraction with the greater denominator has smaller parts. This means it takes more eighths to make a whole than it takes sixths.	3.NF.A.3d
14	A	Dividing evenly into groups is represented by division.	3.OA.A.2
15	B	This is an array with 2 rows and 7 columns	3.OA.A.1, 3.OA.A.3
16	A	2/4 and 3/6 are both equivalent to 1/2	3.NF.A.3a, 3.NF.A.3b
17	24 sq. ft	top portion: $3 \times 6 = 18$ sq. ft and bottom portion $2 \times 3 = 6$ sq ft	3.MD.C.7d
18	D	Anytime the numerator is larger than the denominator, the fraction will be larger than 1. This can also be seen on a number line.	3.NF.A.3c
19	C	There are 9 columns and 4 rows of canned goods, so Mei-Yin can store $9 \times 4 = 36$ canned goods in her pantry.	3.OA.A.1, 3.OA.A.3
20	A	In months 1 and 2 he ran $25 + 30 = 55$ miles. To have run 75 miles, the third month must have consisted of running $75 - 55 = 20$ miles.	3.OA.D.8
21	D	The shaded region is tiled by 20 squares.	3.MD.C.7a
22	B	If one whole is divided into 4 pieces, it will take two wholes to have 8 pieces.	3.NF.A.3a, 3.NF.A.3b
23	D	$8 \times 6 = 48$	3.OA.A.3
24	C	The other items are either significantly too light or significantly too heavy.	3.MD.A.2
25	B	The parts of the number line between 0 and 1 and 1 and 0 are each divided into three equal parts so the denominator of the fraction is 3. The point is 4 marks to the right of the 0, so the numerator is 4. The line shows the fraction $1\frac{1}{3}$, or $\frac{4}{3}$.	3.NF.A.3a, 3.NF.A.3b

OVERVIEW

For Grade 3, the ELA Common Core Standards focus on understanding texts and being able to identify the main idea contained in a passage. The standards also incorporate ideas about sequencing of events in a story or process, as well as identifying cause and effect relationships between events.

Listed below are the ELA Common Core Standards for Grade 3 that we have identified as "power standards." We consider these standards to be critical to your child's success. Each lesson in this section focuses on a single power standard so that you and your child may practice that standard to achieve mastery. The applicable standards are divided into three categories: Reading—Informational Text; Reading—Literature; and Writing.

Reading—Informational Text

CCSS.ELA-Literacy.RI.3.1: Ask and answer questions to demonstrate understanding of a text, referring explicitly to the text as the basis for the answers.

CCSS.ELA-Literacy.RI.3.2: Determine the main idea of a text; recount the key details and explain how they support the main idea.

CCSS.ELA-Literacy.RI.3.3: Describe the relationship between a series of historical events, scientific ideas or concepts, or steps in technical procedures in a text, using language that pertains to time, sequence, and cause/effect.

CCSS.ELA-Literacy.RI.3.4: Determine the meaning of general academic and domain-specific words and phrases in a text relevant to a *grade 3 topic or subject area.*

Reading—Literature

CCSS.ELA-Literacy.RL.3.1: Ask and answer questions to demonstrate understanding of a text, referring explicitly to the text as the basis for the answers.

CCSS.ELA-Literacy.RL.3.2: Recount stories, including fables, folktales, and myths from diverse cultures; determine the central message, lesson, or moral and explain how it is conveyed through key details in the text.

CCSS.ELA-Literacy.RL.3.3: Describe characters in a story (e.g., their traits, motivations, or feelings) and explain how their actions contribute to the sequence of events

CCSS.ELA-Literacy.RL.3.4: Determine the meaning of words and phrases as they are used in a text, distinguishing literal from nonliteral language.

Writing

CCSS.ELA-Literacy.W.3.2: Write informative/explanatory texts to examine a topic and convey ideas and information clearly.

CCSS.ELA-Literacy.W.3.5: With guidance and support from peers and adults, develop and strengthen writing as needed by planning, revising, and editing.

READING

For the reading standards, Common Core breaks texts into two basic types: (1) Informational Texts, which essentially cover all types of nonfiction; and (2) Literature, which includes stories, drama, and poetry. The following chart from the Common Core Standards Initiative provides a brief overview of the range of text types. For the purposes of assessment, texts are also selected from a broad range of cultures and time periods.

Literature			Informational Text
Stories	Dramas	Poetry	Literary Nonfiction and Historical, Scientific, and Technical Texts
Includes children's adventure stories, folktales, legends, fables, fantasy, realistic fiction, and myth	Includes staged dialogue and brief familiar scenes	Includes nursery rhymes and the subgenres of the narrative poem, limerick, and free verse poem	Includes biographies and autobiographies; books about history, social studies, science, and the arts; technical texts, including directions, forms, and information displayed in graphs, charts, or maps; and digital sources on a range of topics

As practice is the best way to build reading skills, encourage your child to read a variety of literary works and informational texts.

Informational Text

Informational texts include literary nonfiction, such as biographies or memoirs, as well as historical, scientific, and technical texts. They include expository, persuasive, and functional texts in the form of personal essays, opinion pieces, speeches, essays, journalism, and other nonfiction accounts. A variety of types of informational texts is included in this section to give your child practice across a range of genres and subgenres.

Literature

The literature category for grades K-5 includes three main subcategories: stories, dramas, and poetry. Stories may be adventure stories, realistic fiction, folktales and fables, legends and myths, and fantasy. Dramas include the written text that would be used for a play, with dialogue, stage directions, and scenes. Poetry includes nursery rhymes, narrative poems, limericks, and free verse. A variety of stories is included in this section of the book to give your child practice with the genre used most commonly on tests. Because practice is the best way to build reading sk lls, encourage your child to read a variety of literary works.

WRITING

The Common Core Standards for writing are tied closely to reading. Many of the skills your child learns to read effectively are also applicable to their own writing. In general, your child will be asked to write short passages that express a specific viewpoint or support a specific argument. For these writing passages, the emphasis will be on using information, details, and examples to support the main idea or ideas. Your child will also be expected to create writing that flows smoothly, with an introductory sentence or paragraph, a main body, and a closing sentence or paragraph. In addition to writing an effective draft, your child will also be asked to revise, adjust, and improve their own writing and the writing of others.

Another critical element is mastery of basic grammar and mechanics appropriate for his or her grade level. This is shown through your child's own writing, as well as through revising and improving the writing of others.

THE STANDARD

RI.3.1: Ask and answer questions to demonstrate understanding of a text, referring explicitly to the text as the basis for the answers.

What does it mean?

This informational text standard focuses on a child's ability to understand a passage and look for answers to questions in the text. The standard also focuses on the ability to ask a relevant question about a text.

Try this together

Your child probably already has experience with this standard, as being able to answer questions about what is read is an integral part of reading. But it is helpful to consider what types of questions are asked and to help your child look for specific answers in the reading. It is also helpful to have your child think about the questions she or he has about the topic.

Pre-reading can be an important skill for understanding a text and being able to answer questions about it. Before beginning, have your child look at the title. Point out that the title reveals the topic of this text. This will often be the case, particularly with informational texts. Ask your child what he or she already knows about castles. Ask also what he or she would like to learn. This will help prepare your child for what he or she is about to read.

Have your child complete the **K-W-L** chart (or work with your child to complete it). Instruct your child to write what he or she already knows about castles in the first column. Then, things that your child wants to know about castles will go in the second column. These columns can be completed before reading the passage. The final column is for your child to record things that he or she has learned in the passage. This provides a concrete way for a reader to prepare for reading and assess what has been read.

K What I Already Know About Castles	W What I Want to Learn About Castles	L What I Learned About the Castles

When your child has completed the first two columns, he or she is ready to read.

READ Castles Past and Present

When people think of castles, they often think of fairytale places. Movies often show castles as places where princesses lived or where princes hosted huge parties. The reality was much different.

Many castles were built during the Middle Ages. These were dangerous times, and kings often were at war. Some castles were built for kings and their families to live in. But a more important goal for castles was to protect people from an invading army. Knights also often lived in castles when they were preparing for battle. In times of war, many other people from the village would seek shelter in the castle.

The earliest castles were built of wood. Wood was too easily set on fire, though, so soon these early castles were replaced with sturdy structures of stone. High walls and thick stone fences kept out the enemy. Castles were usually surrounded by a moat—a deep river of water—so that armies could not put up ladders and climb over the wall.

The only windows in the castle walls were narrow slits that would allow those within to shoot arrows at an invading army. Having no windows made it dark inside. Some castles also had no flow of air, making them cold, clammy places.

? Quiz

One of the important aspects of the standards is to not only answer the question, but also being able to identify where the answer is found. As you answer the questions, work with your child to find the part of the text where the answer is found. Students should answer the questions using complete sentences.

1. What were the Middle Ages like?

   _____

   _____

2. What was the most important purpose that castles served?

_____

_____

3. What is a moat? Why did castles have moats?

_____

_____

4. How did castles change over time?

_____

_____

5. What do you think it would have been like to live in a castle in the Middle Ages? Use details from the passage to support your answer.

_____

_____

_____

_____

Answers

1. What were the Middle Ages like?

   The Middle Ages were dangerous times during which people were often at war. (See paragraph 2.) This question focuses on the context of the passage. Some readers are good about focusing on the main idea or topic—in this case, castles—but they ignore the surrounding information.

2. What was the most important purpose that castles served?

   The main purpose of castles was to protect people from armies. (See paragraph 2.) This question requires readers to go beyond identifying an answer to synthesize/analyze information to determine what is most important.

3. What is a moat? Why did castles have moats?

   A moat is a deep waterway built around the castle. They were used to keep armies from putting up ladders and climbing over the castle wall. (See paragraph 3.) This question helps assess whether students are understanding vocabulary that is introduced in the text. (As such, it integrates with RI.3.4.)

4. How did castles change over time?

   The first castles were wood. Later castles were built of stone. (See paragraph 4.) This question requires students to compare one thing or idea to another.

5. What do you think it would have been like to live in a castle? Use details from the passage to support your answer.

   Answers will vary but should use details to support the answer. This question encourages your child to synthesize the information presented to come to a conclusion. It also requires your child give an opinion and identify facts from the text to back up their opinion.

Extra practice #1

Revisit the **K-W-L** chart. Which information in the "W" column was answered by this passage? Are there other questions that the passage raised that your child would like to know? Encourage your child to come up with at least one question.

1. Have your child complete the last column of the **K-W-L** chart. Your child should add at least three things that they learned from this passage.
2. If possible, help your child find an article that answers the question they identified in question #1. The Internet may be a possible source of information.

Extra practice #2

To help your child work on the skills assessed by this standard, try this activity:

1. Ask your child to draw what they think a castle from the Middle Ages would look like. Have them include as many details from the passage as possible.
2. When your child has finished the drawing, have him or her write a caption describing the picture.
3. Encourage your child to tell you what parts of the passage are shown in the picture.
4. Use the Internet or library to find pictures of castles built during the Middle Ages. Ask your child to find a castle that best illustrates the ideas in this passage.

As you read books with your child, ask questions about what he or she is reading. Try to ask questions that focus not only on the concrete facts of the text but that also require your child to make comparisons and inferences. Encourage your child to ask questions about what he or she is reading, both before beginning to read and after the reading has been completed.

THE STANDARD

RI.3.2: *Determine the main idea of a text; recount the key details and explain how they support the main idea.*

What does it mean?

This standard focuses on a child's ability to understand the main idea of an informational text, such as something they would read in social studies or science. Questions related to the standard may ask about the main idea of a passage as a whole or of a section, paragraph, or other part of the passage.

Try this together

Let's take a short informational text about rabbits as an example of the kind of informational text your child might encounter in school. Questions follow the passage. A teacher might assign these types of questions to assess whether your child understands the main idea of the passage and its components parts.

Before trying this exercise with your child, read through the passage and the questions that follow. Then have your child read the passage aloud to you. Have your child read the passage twice. The first read-through should just be to familiarize your child with the passage. Then, have your child read the text again. Explain that in this reading, he or she should focus on the main ideas. To find the main idea, have your child answer these questions: "What is the passage mostly about?" and "What is the author trying to tell me?" Stop and ask your child these questions after each paragraph.

After reading the entire passage, have your child answer the questions that follow the text. Each of these questions focuses on the main idea of the passage and its component parts. When answering the questions, have your child look back at the text. Referring to the text when answering questions—regardless of the types of questions—can be an integral part of reading success. Students should answer the questions using complete sentences.

 ## Pet Rabbits

Rabbits can make very good pets. In fact, people have been keeping rabbits as pets for hundreds of years!

Like dogs, cats, and even people, not all rabbits are the same. Some rabbits are playful. Some are loyal and friendly. Rabbits are smart. They can learn to respond to their names and to use a litter box.

Like any other pet, rabbits require care. Before getting a rabbit, people need to make sure they will be able to take care of it. This means knowing someone who can take care of the rabbit when you are away. It also means making sure you have a place that a rabbit can stay.

Bunny Care

Pet rabbits need a place to call home. A rabbit should have a cage of his or her own. The cage should be big enough so that the rabbit can hop about. The cage should also have a place for a water bottle, food dish, and bedding. If you have more than one rabbit, you will need a bigger cage.

Unless the cage is very big, your pet bunny will need to be let out to exercise. Some owners set aside a corner or section of the room for their rabbits. It is important to look carefully to make sure the rabbit cannot get hurt. Rabbits love to chew. Electrical wires or telephone cords might be tempting for a rabbit looking for something to chew on. It is important to make sure that these are out of reach of your rabbit.

Rabbits should have access to water at all times. Most people clip a water bottle to the side of the cage. Rabbits eat almost any vegetable, but usually it is better to give them rabbit food. This food will provide them with the diet they need to stay healthy. You can give your rabbit a treat though. Most rabbits love carrots, broccoli, apple slices, or other fruits and vegetables. Do not feed your rabbit lettuce, cabbage, potato, or onions. They can upset a rabbit's tummy.

Like any other animal, a rabbit should have regular check-ups. Your vet can help give you tips on keeping your rabbit healthy. A healthy rabbit is a happy rabbit. A healthy rabbit can be a friend for many years.

Quiz

1. What is the passage mostly about?

   _____

   _____

2. What is the author trying to tell you?

   _____

   _____

3. Which sentence in the second paragraph tells the main idea of paragraph 2?

   _____

   _____

4. What is the main idea of paragraph 6 (the second to last paragraph)?

   _____

   _____

5. Write a sentence describing the main idea of the section "Bunny Care." Then, find at least two details that support this main idea.

   _____

   _____

   _____

✓ Answers

1. What is the passage mostly about?

   Pet rabbits and how to care for them. This question asks children to look at and think about the main idea of the entire passage as a whole. Point out that the author has told the reader that the passage will be about pet rabbits in the very first sentence. Authors often present the main idea at the beginning of the article.

2. What is the author trying to tell you?

   Rabbits make good pets, but they need to be taken care of. This is another question that gets at the main idea of the passage. It focuses on the main idea of the article and then expands beyond "pet rabbits" to focus on what it is about pet rabbits that the author wants the reader to know. There is more than one main idea in this passage: the first part of the passage focuses on the fact that rabbits make good pets; the second part focuses on how to take care of a rabbit.

3. Which sentence in the second paragraph tells the main idea of paragraph 2?

   The first sentence tells the main idea. "Like dogs, cats, and even people, not all rabbits are the same" is the main idea of this paragraph. Just as the main idea of a passage can usually be found at the beginning, the main idea of a paragraph is often the first sentence. In this paragraph, the first sentence tells the main idea: "Like dogs, cats, and even people, not all rabbits are the same." Point out to your child that the other sentences are supporting details. They tell some of the ways that rabbits are different from one another.

4. What is the main idea of paragraph 6 (the second to last paragraph)?

   Rabbits need to have water and the right type of food to stay healthy. This is an example of a paragraph in which the main idea is not explicitly stated. Ask your student, "What is this paragraph mostly about?" (food and water). "What is the author trying to tell you?" (Rabbits need to have water and the right type of food to stay healthy.) All of the sentences in this paragraph support this main idea. They tell how to make sure a rabbit has water and the right type of food.

5. Write a sentence describing the main idea of the section "Bunny Care." Then, find at least two details that support this main idea.

   Having a pet rabbit means taking care of it. The bunny will need a cage to live in. It will also need exercise, food, and water. Bunny care will also require taking it to a veterinarian to keep the rabbit healthy. This question asks students to state the main idea of an entire section. This goes beyond the main idea of a specific paragraph, but readers can determine this with the same two questions they have used to identify the main idea of the passage as a whole and an individual paragraph within this passage. Note that the subtitle helps to identify the main idea. Help your child see how the paragraphs and sentences within this section work together to support the main idea.

Extra practice

To help your child work on the skills assessed by this standard, try this activity:

1. Ask your child to reread the passage.
2. Then, have your child use the information to create a pamphlet on rabbit care. Your child should draw a picture for the pamphlet and include the main ideas about what is important for someone taking care of a pet bunny.

Through this activity your child will be directly practicing the skills listed in the standard. To develop the pamphlet, your child will have to identify and apply the main ideas, answering the questions, "What is the article mostly about?" and "What is the author trying to tell me?"

THE STANDARD

RI.3.3: Describe the relationship between a series of historical events, scientific ideas or concepts, or steps in technical procedures in a text, using language that pertains to time, sequence, and cause/effect.

What does it mean?

This informational text standard focuses on a child's ability to understand the relationship between key ideas. Questions may focus on the steps of a process, the chronological order in which things occur, or cause-and-effect relationships.

Try this together

One part of this standard focuses on the order of things, such as the steps in a process or procedure. Encourage your child to look for hints about when things are to occur or when they did occur. Words like *first, then*, or *finally* often provide valuable clues both for the steps of a process and for chronological order. In a historical passage, your child might also look at the dates to determine the order of events.

The standard also focuses on cause-and-effect relationships. Understanding cause and effect requires going beyond the order in which things happen to determine whether something that happened earlier *caused* or *influenced* the later event. Asking an "If____, then _____" type of question can help your child determine this. ("If I save my money, then I can buy a new book.")

Let's look at a "how-to" passage to focus on the elements of this standard. This passage includes both the steps of a process and cause-and-effect relationships.

 ## Growing Your Own

Having a garden is a fun hobby. You can get fresh vegetables any time you want. It is also often cheaper to grow your own vegetables and herbs than to buy them in the store.

The first thing you need to do is to find a place to grow them. Some people plant huge gardens in their backyards. You can also plant vegetables in pots on a patio or balcony or plant herbs in a window box right outside the kitchen window.

You will need to decide what types of herbs or veggies you want to grow. If you have room, try planting several different vegetables. You can plant lettuce or other salad greens, tomatoes, and carrots all in the same garden. Basil, parsley, and other herbs take up much less room. These herbs might be better choices if you only have a patio.

To plant herbs, you will need seeds, soil, and one or more pots. You can find these at a garden store or order them online. Put soil into your pot. Fill the pot with soil until it is about three-quarters full. Then sprinkle the seeds into the pot. Cover with more soil. Then, put the pot in a sunny place.

It is important to remember to water your seeds. Most herbs grow when the soil is moist, but not overly wet. If you add too much water too often, the plants can drown. Putting your finger in the soil can help you determine whether your plants need watering. (Remember to wash your hands after touching the plant or soil.)

With the right mix of sunshine and water, your seeds will turn into food!

? Quiz

1. What is the first step that you need to take to grow herbs or vegetables?

   _____

2. When should you check the soil?

   _____

   _____

3. What happens when you water a plant too often?

   _____

   _____

4. What two things are needed for plants to grow?

   _____

   _____

5. Identify the steps that you need to take in order to grow herbs in a pot.

   _____

   _____

   _____

   _____

 Answers

1. What is the first step that you need to take to grow herbs or vegetables?
   Find a place to grow them. The standard addresses chronological order or steps in a process. This question asks children to identify the first step. Point out that the author uses the word "first" to help show this as the beginning of a process.

2. When should you check the soil?

   Before giving it water. This question is asking about chronological order, but it also is related to cause and effect. Because the text does not explicitly say when to check the soil, answering the question requires the reader to understand why you would check the soil.

3. What happens if a plant gets too much water?

   It can drown. This question is a follow-up to question 2. It is asking about cause and effect. Having too much water is the cause; causing the plant to drown or die is the effect.

4. What two things are needed for plants to grow?

   Sunshine and water. This question also asks about cause and effect. The desired effect is for your plants to grow. The two things that will cause this are sunshine and water, as shown in the last sentence of this passage. If the plants get water and sunshine, then they will grow.

5. Identify the steps that you need to take in order to grow herbs in a pot.

   (1) Get seeds, soil, and a pot. (2) Fill the pot until it is about ¾ full. (3) Sprinkle seeds into the pot. (4) Cover with more soil. (5) Put the pot in a sunny place. (6) Water as needed. This focuses on the steps in a process. To meet this part of the standard, students need to understand the order in which things are done and be able to translate the paragraph into written steps. Return to the passage with your child and point to each of the steps.

Extra practice

To help your child work on the skills assessed by this standard, try this activity:

1. Explain that you are going to show how to plant herbs to a small child who cannot read.

2. Then, ask your child to create a series of illustrations showing the steps that should be taken to grow an herb garden. Use paragraphs 4 and 5 as a guide. Have your child number each of the illustrations.

3. Then, have your child write an "If . . . then . . ." sentence, such as "If the plant gets _____, then it will _____."

Through this activity your child will be directly practicing the skills listed in the standard. He or she will be identifying the steps of the process and a cause-and-effect relationship.

THE STANDARD

RI.3.4: Determine the meaning of general academic and domain-specific words and phrases in a text relevant to a grade 3 topic or subject area.

What does it mean?

This informational text standard focuses on a child's ability to understand vocabulary. The standard focuses on general academic and domain-specific words and phrases. *General academic words,* sometimes called Tier 2 words, are more likely to appear in written texts than in speech. They can include subtle or precise ways to say relatively simple things. An example at the third-grade level might be *speed* or *rush* in place of *run.* General academic words can appear across many different types of texts, both informational and literary in nature.

In contrast, *domain-specific* words are specific to a field of study. They may introduce a new idea or concept within the text. Understanding these words often requires students to look for clues within the text itself. The passage on castles included for standard RI.3.1, for instance, introduced students to the word *moat.* Domain-specific words may also be part of a glossary or defined in a footnote.

This standard is related to other general vocabulary standards that are part of the Vocabulary Acquisition and Use section of Common Core Language skills. The standard is sometimes tested in connection with those other standards, which are included here for easy reference:

L.3.4 Determine or clarify the meaning of unknown and multiple-meaning word and phrases based on grade 3 reading and content, choosing flexibly from a range of strategies.

- *L.3.4a:* Use sentence-level context as a clue to the meaning of a word or phrase.
- *L.3.4b:* Determine the meaning of the new word formed when a known affix is added to a known word (e.g., *agreeable/disagreeable comfortable/uncomfortable, care/careless, heat/preheat*).
- *L.3.4c:* Use a known root word as a clue to the meaning of an unknown word with the same root (e.g., *company, companion*).
- *L.3.4d:* Use glossaries or beginning dictionaries, both print and digital, to determine or clarify the precise meaning of key words and phrases.

L.3.5: Demonstrate understanding of figurative language, word relationships and nuances in word meanings.

- **L.3.5a:** Distinguish the literal and nonliteral meanings of words and phrases in context (e.g., *take steps*).
- **L.3.5b:** Identify real-life connections between words and their use (e.g., describe people who are *friendly* or *helpful*).
- **L.3.5c:** Distinguish shades of meaning among related words that describe states of mind or degrees of certainty (e.g., *knew, believed, suspected, heard, wondered*).

As you can see from the vocabulary-related standards, success in this area requires students to be able to decipher word meaning using the context in which it is used and knowledge of root words and affixes (prefixes and suffixes). Students also will need to recognize the figurative use of language. (Figurative language involves the use of words or phrases in a way that is not their literal, or dictionary, meaning. Figurative language may include exaggeration, similes, metaphors, etc. Because figurative language is more commonly associated with literary texts, it is addressed in that section of this book. See RL.3.4 for more information.)

Try this together

Let's look at how students can use skills to decipher the meaning of unfamiliar vocabulary terms by looking at an informational text about the island country of Madagascar. By intent, this passage includes vocabulary terms at a level that is slightly higher than third grade, including both general academic and domain-specific words. Ask your child to underline unfamiliar words as he or she reads the passage.

After your child has read the passage, look back together at the words he or she has underlined. Then talk about how you can figure out their meaning. Some of the words may be defined in the text; for others, there might be context clues within the text that can help children figure them out. The questions below are intended to check a child's ability to use various skills to determine word meaning.

 Plants and Animals of Madagascar

Madagascar is an island off the coast of southern Africa. This huge island is far from the nearest land. Because of this, Madagascar's plants and animals are different from those found in other parts of the world. In fact, almost three of every four species of plants and animals in Madagascar are unique to the island.

Lemurs are one group of animals found only in Madagascar. Lemurs are primates, a group of animals that also includes apes, monkeys, and humans. There are 60 different types of lemurs in Madagascar! None of these species is found anywhere else, at least naturally. (You might be able to see a lemur at zoos in other places.) The fossa is another animal that lives only in Madagascar. The fossa is a carnivore, or meat-eating animal. It looks like a cross between a dog and a wild cat. Madagascar is also home to the dwarf hippopotamus, the largest mammal on the island. There are also many types of fish, butterflies, and other insects, as well as some unique species of frogs not found anywhere else on earth.

Madagascar also has many plant species. There are a thousand different types of orchids, a beautiful flower that only grows where it is warm and wet. Huge palm trees grow along the coast of the island. In the middle are deciduous trees, a type of tree that loses its leaves in the winter. The southwestern part of Madagascar gets little rainfall. Many of the plants and trees look like cacti. A strange tree of Madagascar is the baobab. Baobabs have fruit. The baobab has a thick short trunk that allows the tree to store lots of water. This allows it to thrive where it is dry.

? Quiz

1. What does the word *species* mean? What part of the text provides clues about this word's meaning?

   _____

   _____

2. What is a primate?

   _____

   _____

3. The text says, "None of these species is found anywhere else, at least naturally." What does the word *naturally* mean here?

   _____

   _____

4. What is a carnivore?

   _____

   _____

5. The text says, "It looks like a cross between a dog and a wild cat." Look at the following dictionary definitions:

   cross: (1) cross-shaped symbol; (2) mix of two breeds; (3) go across; (4) angry

   Which definition fits the way *cross* is used in this passage?

   _____

6. What is a mammal?

   _____

   _____

7. What is an orchid?

   _____

   _____

8. What happens to deciduous trees?

   _____

   _____

9. Describe a baobab.

_____

_____

10. What does *thrive* mean?

_____

_____

✓ Answers

1. What does the word *species* mean? How can you tell?

   Species *is a type or kind of something, such as an animal. The last sentence in the first paragraph relates* species *to plants and animals. You can replace this word with the word type or kind. This requires looking at the word in context. The text does not specifically define* species, *but it does refer to it in the context of plants or animals. The first paragraph is talking about the many different types of plants and animals. Note that the word is repeated in the second paragraph. Domain-specific words are often repeated to provide additional context clues and reinforce meaning. If your child is having trouble figuring out word meaning, tell him or her to look for places where the word is repeated.*

2. What is a primate?

   A primate is a type of animal. The type (or order) includes apes, monkeys, and humans. This is an example of a domain-specific word that is defined in the text. Here, the meaning of the word can be inferred from the examples of primates that are given.

3. The text says, "None of these species is found anywhere else, at least naturally." What does the word *naturally* mean here?

   Naturally *means as part of nature, without human interference or aid. This is an example of a word that has a root word that can help determine meaning. Help your child see the word* nature *within the word. The meaning is also reinforced by the surrounding context. The following sentence says that lemurs might be found in zoos; in other words, not in nature or naturally.*

4. What is a carnivore?

   A carnivore is an animal that eats meat. Here, the word carnivore is specifically defined. The text explicitly says that it is a meat-eating animal. The text says, "It looks like a cross between a dog and a wild cat."

5. The text says, "It looks like a cross between a dog and a wild cat." Look at the following dictionary definitions:

   cross: (1) cross-shaped symbol; (2) mix of two breeds; (3) go across; (4) angry

   Which definition fits the way *cross* is used in this passage?

   The correct answer is (2) mix of two breeds. This is an example of how to figure out the meaning of a multiple-meaning word by looking at the context. One of the tools that might help your child do this is to replace the word being defined with each of the definitions to

see which one makes sense. It may be helpful at this point to remind your child that just because a word is familiar, it does not mean that they will know what the word means when they read it; some words have many meanings.

6. What is a mammal?

   A mammal is a type of animal. From the context, a student should be able to tell that a mammal is a type of animal. The dwarf hippopotamus is an animal and the text says that it is a mammal.

7. What is an orchid?

   An orchid is a tropical flower. As with the word carnivore earlier, the definition of orchid is provided following the introduction of the word.

8. What happens to deciduous trees?

   They lose their leaves in winter. This is an example of a question that focuses on how the word affects meaning. The text answers the question fairly explicitly.

9. Describe a baobab.

   A baobab is a tree with a thick trunk and fruit. This type of question assesses not only the basic definition—a baobab is a tree—but also the ability to relate the word to its description.

10. What does *thrive* mean?

    Thrive *means to live or survive. Unlike some of the other words that are clearly defined in the text, this question requires students to look at the context. If your child is struggling with this type of question, have him or her visualize what is happening in the passage. Say: "The baobab tree can store water, and water is needed for a tree to live. What does that tell you about the meaning of the word* thrive?"

Extra practice

Many of the vocabulary-related questions will ask questions to see whether students can relate the meaning of the word to another context. Here are a few examples for your child to practice with the words he or she has just learned in this passage:

1. A lemur has the most in common with which of the following animals?

   a. chimpanzee   *b. dog*   *b. frog*   *d. hippo*

2. Which of the following is unique? (check all that apply)

   a. your fingerprint   *c. a pencil*

   b. a library book   *d. a snowflake*

3. Are deciduous trees unique to Madagascar?

   yes   *no*

4. Is a butterfly a primate?

   yes   *no*

5. Name an animal, other than those mentioned in the passage, that is a carnivore.

☑ Answers

1. a; 2. a, d; 3. no; 4. no; 5. Answers will vary. Possible answers: dog, cat, lion, eagle. (Any meat-eating animal would be correct.)

As you read with your child, practice the skills here to figure out word meaning. Remind your child of these steps:

1. Look for context clues. Begin with the adjacent words and phrases and then move to nearby phrases and sentences.
2. Visualize the word or what is being described to help put the word in context.
3. Look for root words. Are there words that sound or look similar to the unfamiliar word?
4. Consider the various meanings of multiple-meaning words. Does the first meaning that comes to mind make sense in the sentence?
5. Look for other places that an unfamiliar word is used. If it is used more than once in the text, the other places might help confirm its meaning.

Look for opportunities to further explore word meaning with your child. Encourage your child to use the word in a sentence. Or ask a question that helps your child relate the word to what he or she knows (e.g., Which trees in our yard are deciduous?).

As children read, they will naturally build their vocabulary. Being able to use a variety of strategies to determine word meaning will help them meet the goals of the standard and be better readers across all disciplines.

THE STANDARD

RL.3.1: Ask and answer questions to demonstrate understanding of a text, referring explicitly to the text as the basis for the answers.

What does it mean?

This standard focuses on a child's ability to ask relevant questions about a literary work. Questions might focus on the characters or their motivations, on the setting, or on the plot. The standard also addresses a child's ability to answer these questions by giving a detail or example from the passage.

Try this together

As with nonfiction texts, preparing to read is an important step for reading a passage. Before reading a book, have your child look at the table of contents, chapter headings, and illustrations. What does the book look like it will be about?

If a passage includes an illustration, encourage your child to look at the illustration before reading. Similar predictions can help during reading. Encourage your child to pause after sections of the passage to make a prediction about what will happen next.

Visualizing is another important reading strategy. Have your child pause to think about what the scene or character looks like.

Finally, asking and answering questions—the focus of this standard—is integral to understanding. Having children form their own questions encourages active learning. It may also help readers to recognize when they are confused about something, whether it is a twist in the plot or an unfamiliar word.

Now that you have these three strategies in mind, you are ready to "pre-read" the passage with your child. Begin by having your child look at the illustrations for this passage. Ask, "What do you think the story might be about?" "What clues do you see that support this prediction?" Then have your child read the title. "Does this confirm your predictions?"

After a brief discussion, have your child read the passage aloud to you. Encourage your child to stop periodically to predict what will happen next. Also, encourage your child to ask questions about the passage by modeling this yourself (e.g., "I wonder whether Hannah will find any customers." or "Why did Joey say he wasn't home?").

 ## The Pet-Sitters' Club

It began fairly simply. Mrs. Deegan sent an email to the members of our neighborhood association, asking if anyone had kids who wanted to housesit. My mother, who is a bit of a night owl, happened to be online when the email came through. She replied without even asking us. The next morning she announced that we had a job.

"You know Cheezo?"

Of course we did. Cheezo used to visit our patio to look in the door at our cats. Caesar and Romeo were strictly indoor cats, and they didn't like it much when Cheezo lounged on the patio. Jake and I just nodded at Mom.

"Well, Mrs. Deegan is going to be out of town, so she's looking for someone to go over and feed Cheezo. I signed you guys up."

"Okay," I said. "I love Cheezo."

It wasn't really true. After all, Cheezo bugged our cats, who hissed at him through the door, but I didn't want Mom to give the job to someone else.

The next day we went over and met Cheezo and picked up the key from Mrs. Deegan. She was only gone for a weekend that first time, but she left for a week the next month and for ten days in the summer. Pretty soon, Jake and I were taking care of Cheezo on a regular basis. I also grew to love Cheezo. He was lonely without Mrs. Deegan and wanted me to pet him. I'd bring a book and sit on her couch with him on my lap.

That summer, Mrs. Deegan told her next door neighbors, the Clarks, that we were taking care of Cheezo. Their son Colin was about to start college, and they needed someone to let Hannah out in the afternoon. "You just need to let her out for a few minutes when you get home from school," said Mrs. Clark. "The yard is fenced in, so she won't go anywhere. Then just let her back in."

Taking care of Hannah was an even easier job than feeding Cheezo. It was also more fun. On warm fall days, we'd hang around in the Clarks' yard and play catch with Hannah. We were in no hurry to go home and start our homework. On snowy days, we'd throw snowballs, and Hannah would try to catch them. Her excitement turned to surprise when she caught a snowball and it crumbled in her mouth.

It was Thanksgiving break when we got our next customer. The Gomez family went away for the long weekend and asked us to feed their hamster and two fish. "Could you also take out the trash on Friday evening?" Mr. Gomez asked. "There will be an extra five bucks in it for you."

"You've got quite a business started," my dad said that Friday as Jake and I headed out. I was off to feed Cheezo while Jake stopped by the Gomezes. Then we were going to meet at the Clarks to play with Hannah. "You should start marketing your services."

"What do you mean?" asked Jake. He was usually pretty quiet, but if there was one thing he loved it was money. I once opened the drawer next to his bed and it was stuffed with the green stuff!

"Well, you should make a flyer and put it in our neighbors' mailboxes. I'm sure Mrs. Deegan, the Clarks, and Mr. Gomez would all be willing to vouch for you."

When I got home later, I found Jake at the computer working on a flyer. "What do you think?" he asked. He had found pictures of a boy playing with a dog and two kids with a hamster. It had a list of our current customers and the work we had done for them, as well as our address and phone number.

"We need a name," said Jake.

"What's wrong with Jake and Sophia?" I asked.

"It doesn't sound like a business. We need a name for our pet-sitting business."

"How about Jake and Sophia's Pet-Sitting Business?" I suggested.

Jake shook his head. "It has to be catchy—something that sounds like a real business, not just a couple of kids."

We were staring at the computer screen as if it would have the answer when our dad strolled by. "How's my pet sitters' club?" he asked.

"That's it!" said Jake, as he typed "THE PET-SITTERS' CLUB" in capital letters across the top of the flyer. "Like it?"

And so our business was officially born.

? Quiz

1. How did Sophia feel about the first pet-sitting job? Why?

   _____

   _____

2. How did Sophia's feelings about Cheezo change during the story?

   _____

   _____

3. Were Jake and Sophia good pet-sitters? Give details from the story to support your answer.

   _____

   _____

   _____

4. Do you think the pet-sitting business will grow? Why or why not?

   _____

   _____

5. What can you tell about the setting (where the story takes place)?

   _____

   _____

 Answers

1. *How did Sophia feel about the first pet sitting job? Why?*
   Sophia wanted to pet-sit, but she wasn't sure she liked Cheezo. This question requires a student to look back to the story to think about the main character and his or her motivation.

2. *How did Sophia's feelings about Cheezo change during the story?*
   She grew to love Cheezo. This question asks how one of the characters changes or grows.

These types of questions are common because they require a reader to understand the plot of the story and what kind of people the characters are. They often get at the theme, or lesson, of the story.

3. Were Jake and Sophia good pet-sitters? Give details from the story to support your answer.

Yes. They took good care of the animals. Sophia spent time with Cheezo, who enjoyed sitting on her lap. They both also spent time playing with Hannah. You can tell that the owners thought they were good pet-sitters, because they recommended them to other neighbors. This question requires a student to look beyond what is specifically stated in the story. The author does not tell a reader that Jake and Sophia are good pet-sitters. A reader has to make inferences from the information provided. Talk to your child about the information that is provided to answer this question.

4. Do you think the pet-sitting business will grow? Why or why not?

Yes. The people who they are pet-sitting for will recommend them to other people. This question requires students to come to a conclusion based on the evidence and to make a prediction. It reinforces the idea of making predictions during reading, as well and asking questions.

5. What can you tell about the setting (where the story takes place)?

It seems like a suburban neighborhood. You can also tell that the story takes place somewhere with four seasons, because it mentions warm fall days and snowy days. Like question 3, this question requires readers to make inferences. Point out the clues that the author gives about where the story takes place.

Extra practice

To help your child work on the skills assessed by this standard, have your child write a paragraph about what might happen next in the story. Have your child draw a picture to match this next part.

This activity will encourage your child to be a better reader. Having to think about what happens next requires your child to understand the characters and their motivations, as well as the plot. It also reinforces the notion of making predictions, which is an important tool for building the skills identified in Common Core.

THE STANDARD

RL.3.2: Recount stories, including fables, folktales, and myths from diverse cultures; determine the central message, lesson, or moral and explain how it is conveyed through key details in the text.

What does it mean?

This literature standard focuses on a child's ability to understand the theme, or lesson, of a story and to identify important parts of the story that express the theme.

Try this together

Let's take this short version of the American folktale of John Henry as an example of the kind of literature your child might encounter in school. To address this reading standard, a teacher might ask questions such as the ones that follow the story, or assign them as homework. We have provided possible answers in the "Answers" section, along with an explanation of how the questions connect to the standard in the "What's the point?" section.

Before trying this exercise with your child, read through the story and the questions that follow it yourself. Then have your child read the story aloud to you and the answer the questions that follow. Talk about the answers together. Help your child notice how he or she can find answers to questions by looking back at the story.

 ## John Henry

In the 1860s, war between the North and South tore America apart. After the war it was time to rebuild. Railroads were built to stretch across the country. Building railroads was hard work. Strong men broke through rocks with hammers and steel to make way for railroad tracks. The strongest steel driver of all was John Henry. They say he was born with a hammer in his hand. That might not be true. What is true is that he lived with a hammer in his hand.

John Henry could break through solid rock faster than any man. One day he faced a machine. It was a hammering machine powered by steam. John Henry was proud. He did not want a machine to take his place. He challenged the machine's driver to a contest. They would see who could tunnel through a mountain faster

The contest began at the break of day. John Henry's hammer pounded like thunder. His hammer blows were so loud and strong, the earth shook for miles around. Crowds gathered to watch the steel driving man do what no one else could. But right next to him was the hammering machine. It was pounding too.

For hours and hours both man and machine hammered. As the sun began to set, John Henry broke through his tunnel. He was covered in sweat and dust. The machine broke through next. John Henry had won, but he paid a price. He fell to his knees. His muscles were strong. His will was stronger. But his heart could beat no longer. And there he died, with his hammer in his hand.

? Quiz

1. Which detail from the first paragraph best describes the work of a steel driver?

_____

2. What do these lines tell us about John Henry: "They say he was born with a hammer in his hand. That might not be true. What is true is that he lived with a hammer in his hand."

_____

_____

3. There is a contest in the story. What is the reason for the contest?

_____

_____

4. The last paragraph of the story shows the theme of the story. Which sentence in the paragraph best expresses the theme? Why do you think so?

_____

_____

5. The story of John Henry is famous. His contest with the machine has been sung about and told for more than a hundred years. Why do you think people keep telling this story? Use details from the story to support your answer.

_____

_____

_____

_____

 Answers

1. Which detail from the first paragraph best describes the work of a steel driver?
   "Strong men broke through rocks with hammers and steel to make way for railroad tracks." This question requires students to point directly to details in the story, an important aspect of the standard.

2. What do these lines below tell us about John Henry: "They say he was born with a hammer in his hand. That might not be true. What is true is that he lived with a hammer in his hand"?
   These lines paint a picture of a person who is strong and hard-working. This question is

slightly more difficult that the first, in that it asks students to both recall important, specific details and begin to formulate how these details help portray the main character.

3. There is a contest in the story. What is the reason for the contest?

   John Henry wanted to show he was better than the machine and couldn't be replaced. This question requires students to identify a key detail that has a direct connection to the central message of the story.

4. The last paragraph of the story shows the theme of the story. Which sentence in the paragraph best expresses the theme? Why do you think so?

   "John Henry had won, but he paid a price." The line expresses the theme that a person can work just as hard, if not better, than a machine. This question first requires students to identify the theme and then determine how an important detail supports this theme.

5. The story of John Henry is famous. His contest with the machine has been sung about and told for more than a hundred years. Why do you think people keep telling this story?

   Answers will vary. Some students may say that people keep telling the story because it is part of our American folk heritage. Others may say that it remains popular because it presents a character who is incredibly powerful and strong-willed. Still others may say that the story is entertaining. Accept answers that are well-supported. This question is high-level. It calls on students to speculate about the story from different angles.

Extra practice

To help your child work on the skills assessed by this standard, try this activity:

1. First ask your child to reread the story of John Henry.
2. Then ask your child to create an illustrated, comic-book style version of the story that uses text boxes and dialogue bubbles to move the action forward. The illustrated version should have only five panels or pages that should focus on the most important parts of the story, especially those that support the central message.
3. Tell your child their illustrated story needs to have a cover that includes a title that expresses the theme of the story.

Through this activity, your child will be directly practicing the skills listed in the standard. He or she will recount the story by telling and illustrating it themselves; will focus on key details by fitting them into five illustrated pages; and will identify the central message by coming up with a title that describes the theme of the story. Praise your child's work, explaining exactly what skills he or she used to complete the illustrated story.

THE STANDARD

RL.3.3: Describe characters in a story (e.g., their traits, motivations, or feelings) and explain how their actions contribute to the sequence of events.

What does it mean?

This literature standard focuses on a child's ability to understand the characters of a story. Questions focus on the character traits or qualities of main characters, how these character traits affect what happens, and how characters may change during the course of the story.

Try this together

Your child is probably familiar with fiction, but it is fairly uncommon for a third-grade student to read many dramas. Since dramas are included on standardized tests that assess Common Core standards, we have included an excerpt from a play for this standard.

Explain to your child that reading a drama is a lot like reading a story. It is a little different, however, in that all the actions are presented through dialogue. Prepare to read the drama by pointing out that it begins with a very brief description of the setting, and that most of the drama consists of dialogue between three boys.

 ## The Campout

[It is fall. Three boys are hanging out at the elementary school playground as they wait for their moms to pick them up after school. A teacher is standing nearby.]

BEN: Hey, are you going to the campout this weekend? I'm looking for some friends to share a tent with me.

KEVIN: Yep, I'm going. My mom is going to take me this afternoon to get some stuff for it.

BEN (turning to Diego): Are you going?

DIEGO: Umm. . . I'm not sure.

KEVIN: Your mom said you were. At least that's what my mom said.

DIEGO: Well, I'm not sure.

BEN: Oh, come on. You have to go! It's going to be so much fun! And you always have the best stories for the campfire.

KEVIN: Yeah, your scary stories are the best!

DIEGO: Well, my dad can't go with me this year. Are your dads going?

KEVIN: Nope! This will be my first campout without Dad.

BEN: My dad is going. He said they're going to assign two or three boys to each grown-up, since this is the first campout without everyone's parents, so you don't have to worry about not having your dad there, Diego.

KEVIN (kidding): You're not scared, are you, Mr. Scary Storyteller?

DIEGO (looking down): Ummm, well, maybe just a little.

KEVIN: Is that why you don't want to go?

DIEGO: I guess so. I mean, I'm not usually scared, but it's dark at those camps. At home I sleep with my closet light on. Now you probably think I'm a wimp.

KEVIN: No, I don't think you're a wimp. I'm scared sometimes, too. At our last campout I couldn't sleep after you told that ghost story. It was sooo scary! My mom's gonna buy me a camp light that I can keep on in case I get scared this year.

BEN: Problem solved! We can share a tent and Kevin's light. With all three of us there, it won't be scary. It will just be fun! Besides, my dad will be there. If we get really scared we can always sleep in his tent.

KEVIN: I'll be fine as long as you don't tell any of your super-scary stories.

DIEGO: Well, I just read one the other day that would be perfect for a campfire! As long as we have each other, I guess it won't be too scary.

Quiz

1. How is this campout going to be different from past campouts? How does this affect how Diego feels about the campout?

   _____

   _____

2. What details show that these boys are good friends?

   _____

   _____

3. What adjective would you use to describe Kevin? What evidence is there to support your choice?

   _____

   _____

   _____

4. How do Diego's feelings about the campout change during the play? Which line from the play shows that his feelings have changed?

   _____

   _____

   _____

5. Ben says, "Problem solved!" What problem is he referring to?

   _____

   _____

✓ Answers

1. How is this campout going to be different from past campouts? How does this affect how Diego feels about the campout?

   Not all parents are going to this campout and the boys are going to sleep in their own tents. This makes Diego nervous. This is central to the play. It focuses on the motivation of the characters, which is an explicit part of the standard, and helps determine whether a reader understands why the characters behave as they do.

2. What details show that these boys are good friends?

   Ben wants the other two boys to share a tent with him. Also, Diego is not afraid to admit that he is scared. When he does, the other two boys are kind. This question provides information about the motivation of the characters and requires readers to find evidence to support the analysis.

3. What adjective would you use to describe Kevin? What evidence is there to support your choice?

   Kevin is sympathetic. He is concerned about Diego and tries to make him feel better about being scared. This question focuses on the traits part of the standard. It also requires readers to find evidence in the play to support their answer.

4. How do Diego's feelings about the campout change during the play? Which line from the play shows that his feelings have changed?

   Diego is scared to go to the campout at the outset of the play. The final line shows that Diego is ready to be the scary story teller again. This question focuses on how the feelings of a character change during the course of events and how the actions of the other characters contribute to the sequence of events, as highlighted in the standard.

5. Ben says, "Problem solved!" What problem is he referring to?

   The problem is that Diego is scared to go camping without his dad. This question assesses whether a reader can relate a specific piece of evidence to a character's traits or motivations.

Extra practice

To help your child work on the skills assessed by this standard, try this activity:

1. First ask your child to reread the play.
2. Then have your child come up with at least two adjectives to describe each of the characters.
3. Finally have your child explain why he or she described the characters as they did. Encourage them to point to specific parts of the play that support their analysis.

Through this activity your child will gain practice describing the characters.

For further practice, have your child reread the passages for the two previous literature standards (RL.3.1 and RL.3.2) and give adjectives to describe each of the characters in these stories. Ask your child to explain the reasons for their descriptions and provide details to support these reasons.

THE STANDARD

RL.3.4: Determine the meaning of words and phrases as they are used in a text, distinguishing literal from nonliteral language.

What does it mean?

This literature standard focuses on a child's understanding of vocabulary, including nonliteral figurative language. In advanced grades, the understanding of vocabulary will include understanding the meaning of figures of speech; here, it focuses primarily on recognizing words or phrases that are used in a nonliteral way—that is, in a way different from the dictionary's definition.

Try this together

To review this standard, we have chosen a poem. Begin by explaining that not all poems rhyme. The following is an example of a free verse poem. It does not rhyme.

Have your child read the poem aloud. Then have your child read the poem again and underline any words that are unfamiliar. As with the lesson for Standard RI.3.4, we will review some of the strategies for understanding difficult vocabulary.

 A Summer Storm

Rumbling thunder,
Darkening clouds,
The first few drops of rain,
A storm is approaching.
Flash of lightning,
Crack of thunder,
Rush of rain,
The storm has arrived.
Loud at first,
Then quieter,
And quieter still,
The storm is moving on.
The sun peeks through the clouds
A red robin steps out
To sip from a clear, pure puddle.
The storm has made its mark.

? Quiz

1. What does *rumbling* mean (Line 1)?

   _____

2. What does *approaching* mean (Line 4)?

   _____

3. Look at the dictionary definitions for the word *crack*.

   Crack: (1) thin break; (2) long, narrow hole or opening; (3) sudden or sharp noise; (4) weakness.

   Which meaning of the word is used in this poem (Line 6)?

   _____

   _____

4. The last stanza begins, "The sun peeks through the clouds." What does this mean?

   _____

   _____

5. What does *pure* mean (Line 15)? Which word in this line is most helpful in understanding this word's meaning?

   _____

   _____

6. In the last line of the poem, it says that "The storm has made its mark." What does this mean?

   _____

   _____

☑ Answers

1. What does *rumbling* mean (Line 1)?

   Rumbling is the deep rolling sound that the thunder is making. This question asks students to determine word meaning based on context. Rumbling is used to describe thunder. If readers don't know the meaning, they should be able to determine from this context that it is the sound the thunder is making in the distance. Point out to your child that one of the best ways to determine word meaning is to look at the closest word. What does the word describe? How does this help you figure out what it means?

2. What does *approaching* mean (Line 4)?

   Coming closer. Like the previous question, this question also asks students to use context to figure out the word's meaning. Figuring out this word may require looking beyond the word right next to it to consider what is happening in the poem. Looking at the stanza as a whole and perhaps the next stanza should enable your child to figure out that the storm is coming closer.

3. Look at the dictionary definitions for the word *crack.*

   Crack: (1) thin break; (2) long, narrow hole or opening; (3) sudden or sharp noise; (4) weakness.

   Which meaning of this word is used in this poem (Line 6)?

   The correct answer is (3) sudden or sharp noise. This question asks the meaning of a word that has several meanings. A good reader will be able to use context to figure out which meaning makes the most sense. Here, the word crack *is associated with thunder. Since* thunder *is a noise,* crack *must also be a noise.*

4. The last stanza begins, "The sun peeks through the clouds." What does this mean?

   The sun is starting to come out. This Common Core standard specifically asks for students to be able to differentiate between literal and nonliteral uses of words. Here the word peek *is used nonliterally. Point out to your child that the sun is not really peeking in a literal way, but understanding what* peek *means can help you determine what is really happening here.*

5. What does *pure* mean (Line 15)? Which word in this line means almost the same thing?

   Pure *means "untouched";* clear *means almost the same thing. In some cases, figuring out word meaning means looking for a synonym. In this case, the other word used to describe the puddle—*clear*—can help a student know what is meant by* pure.

6. In the last line of the poem, it says that "The storm has made its mark." What does this mean?

   There is a change between the way things were before and after the storm. The storm's mark is the puddles. This question asks the meaning of a phrase. Understanding the meaning requires an understanding of what is happening in the poem and how the phrase is used. Again, it is a nonliteral use of the phrase.

As children read, they will naturally build their vocabulary. Being able to use a variety of strategies to determine word meaning will help them meet the goals of the standard and be better readers across all disciplines.

Extra practice

Look back at the passages included for the other reading standards. Have your child reread the passage and underline any unfamiliar words. Then, work with him or her to see if you can figure out the word meanings using some of the strategies that have been introduced:

1. Look for context clues. Begin with the adjacent words and phrases and then move to nearby phrases and sentences.

2. Visualize the word or what is being described to help put the word in context.

3. Look for root words. Are there words that sound or look similar to the unfamiliar word?

4. Consider the various meanings of multiple-meaning words. Does the first meaning that comes to mind make sense in the sentence?

5. Look for other places that an unfamiliar word is used. If it is used more than once in the passage, the other places might help confirm its meaning.

Remind your child that if word meaning cannot be figured out using these strategies, the dictionary or online thesaurus is a good reference. Your child can also use a dictionary to confirm that he or she has correctly figured out the meaning of an unknown word.

Encourage your child to use these strategies in future reading. Although the types of vocabulary used may be very different from one type of text to another, the strategies will remain the same.

THE STANDARD

W.3.2: Write informative/explanatory texts to examine a topic and convey ideas and information clearly.

- *W.3.2a: Introduce a topic and group related information together; include illustrations when useful to aiding comprehension.*
- *W.3.2b: Develop the topic with facts, definitions, and details.*
- *W.3.2c: Use linking words and phrases (e.g., also, another, and, more, but) to connect ideas within categories of information.*
- *W.3.2d: Provide a concluding statement or section.*

What does it mean?

This standard focuses on a child's ability to write a well-organized paragraph or series of paragraphs. It is designed to assess how well a child can organize information, develop a topic by providing appropriate supporting information, and make connections between and among the ideas.

The focus of this writing standard is informational or explanatory types of writing. (Other standards focus on persuasive writing and literary pieces or fiction.) Informational or explanatory pieces are defined as those that convey information to increase readers' knowledge of a topic or their understanding of a procedure or process. Students may draw from what they already know and/or conduct additional research into a topic. Just a few of the many examples of the types of writing that teachers might assign to address this standard include summarizing a book that students have read, explaining the causes and/or effects of a historical event, or describing the steps in a scientific experiment.

As shown in the sub-steps of the W.3.2 writing standard, the writing assesses the basic elements of a paragraph or essay, including the introduction (W.3.2a), body (W.3.2.b), and conclusion (W.3.2d). It also focuses on using linking words and phrases to connect ideas.

Try this together

Regardless of their skill level, all writers get better with practice. Unfortunately, many young writers become overwhelmed when writing is taught all at once. It may help to break down the writing process and focus on one part of the W.3.2 standard at a time. This book will look at how this might be done.

The first challenge is often to think of a topic. For the purposes of this exercise, have your child pick an animal that he or she is interested in. Encourage your child to pick a topic that he or she knows about. If you have a pet, this might be a good choice.

Once your child has selected a topic, he or she will have to think about the key facts that he or she wants to include about this topic. The graphic organizer below, often called an "idea map," can be used to help your child think through some of the facts, definitions, or details to include about the topic. The topic (the name of the animal about which your child is writing) should go in the center circle. Then, in each of the surrounding circles or spokes, have your child write facts, definitions, and details to include about this animal.

Once your child has identified the topic, have him write a topic sentence. The topic sentence tells readers what the paragraph is about.

Then, have your child turn each of the ideas in the spokes of the graphic organizer into a sentence. These will follow the topic sentence. Encourage your child to use linking words to connect ideas.

Finally, have your child write a concluding sentence. Explain that the conclusion should sum up all the ideas presented. It should not introduce new ideas or leave the reader with questions.

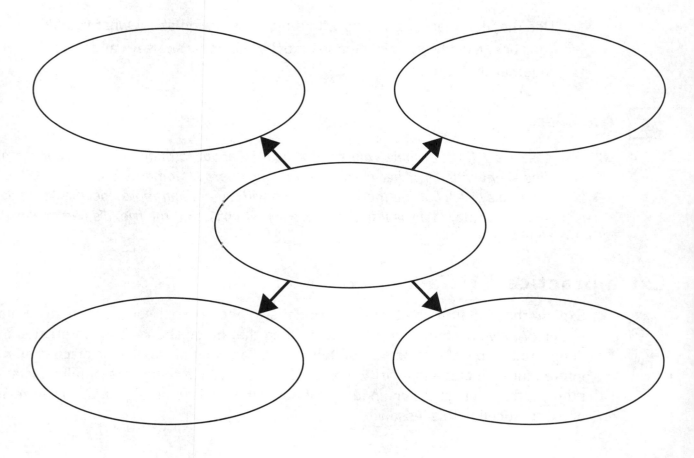

? Quiz

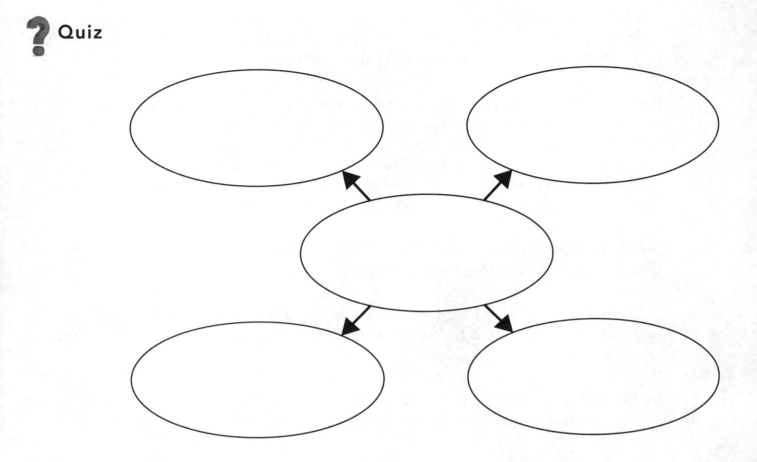

Use the idea map to come up with a plan for writing about what you like most about your best friend. Try to remember exact thing he or she says and does or that you do together than you like.

✓ Answers

Answers will vary widely. Your child should be about to think of some clear memories of time spent with his or her friend. If your child offers statements like "we have fun" or "we like to play," encourage them to come up with something more specific. What games do they like to play? Why is it fun? Is there something about the friend's personality that your child likes?

Extra practice #1: Talk about it

Explain that the first challenge of writing is to decide what you want to say. Help select a topic. Ask your child to think of something that he or she is really interested in. Then, simply talk about the topic. As you talk, reflect on what parts of your discussion might be interesting to include in a written essay. Point out which things are details, facts, and examples that support the main idea. Jot down these ideas on a graphic organizer like the one introduced in this lesson.

Extra practice #2: Read it

You can also help your child become a better writer by focusing on how the writers of their favorite books organize their writing. Have your child find a nonfiction book at his or her level. (This can also be done with the passages included in Reading Informational Text section of this book.) Pick a paragraph from the book or passage you have chosen. With your child, look at how the writer introduces the topic (W.3.2a). Usually, the topic sentence is the first sentence of a paragraph. What does the author say to tell the reader that this will be the topic he or she is writing about? (The introduction of a topic is closely related to the main idea. Review the lesson for RI.3.2 if your child is having difficulty with this.)

Then, discuss how the author expands on the topic (W.3.2b). Help your child identify facts, definitions, and/or details that the author includes. Point out that the facts are groups together to support the main idea(s).

Then look for linking words and phrases (such as also, another, and, more, and but). Make a game out of identifying linking words. Challenge your child to see how many linking words he or she can find. Talk to your child about how these linking words help connect ideas.

Finally, look at how the author concludes the paragraph and/or book. Point out that the writer summarizes the information that he or she has been writing about. No new information is introduced in the conclusion.

THE STANDARD

W.3.5: With guidance and support from peers and adults, develop and strengthen writing as needed by planning, revising, and editing. (Editing for conventions should demonstrate command of Language standards 1-3 up to and including grade 3.)

What does it mean?

This writing standard focuses on a child's ability to improve upon his or her writing. The standard includes strategies for planning one's writing, as well as for revising the writing to make it clearer. The standard also focuses on editing for punctuation, spelling, grammar, and other writing conventions. As such, it is closely related to the Conventions of Standard English standards that are part of the Common Core Language skills. The third-grade standards related to this are highlighted in the sidebar.

L.3.1 Demonstrate command of the conventions of standard English grammar and usage when writing or speaking.

- *L.3.1a* Explain the function of nouns, pronouns, verbs, adjectives, and adverbs in general and their functions in particular sentences.
- *L.3.1b* Form and use regular and irregular plural nouns.
- *L.3.1c* Use abstract nouns (e.g., childhood).
- *L.3.1d* Form and use regular and irregular verbs.
- *L.3.1e* Form and use the simple (e.g., I walked; I walk; I will walk) verb tenses.
- *L.3.1f* Ensure subject-verb and pronoun-antecedent agreement.*
- *L.3.1g* Form and use comparative and superlative adjectives and adverbs, and choose between them depending on what is to be modified.
- *L.3.1h* Use coordinating and subordinating conjunctions.
- *L.3.1i* Produce simple, compound, and complex sentences.

L.3.2 Demonstrate command of the conventions of standard English capitalization, punctuation, and spelling when writing.

- *L.3.2a* Capitalize appropriate words in titles.
- *L.3.2b* Use commas in addresses.
- *L.3.2c* Use commas and quotation marks in dialogue.
- *L.3.2d* Form and use possessives.
- *L.3.2e* Use conventional spelling for high-frequency and other studied words and for adding suffixes to base words (e.g., sitting, smiled, cries, happiness).
- *L.3.2f* Use spelling patterns and generalizations (e.g., word families, position-based spellings,

syllable patterns, ending rules, meaningful word parts) in writing words.
- **L.3.2g** Consult reference materials, including beginning dictionaries, as needed to check and correct spellings.

Try this together

The previous lesson covered part of the planning phase of writing. This phase also includes narrowing down a topic. To help your child do this, have him or her think of a topic that he or she wants to write about. Then have your son or daughter decide what is most interesting about this topic. The graphic organizer on the next page provides a visual image for what narrowing down the topic would look like.

As an example, ask your son or daughter to select a country that he or she wants to learn more about. The name of the country can go on the top line. Explain that you could write an entire book about this country, so you will need to narrow down the topic to something more manageable. Ask your child what about the country he or she finds particularly interesting. Your child might be interested in the people, the culture, or the geography, for instance. Selecting one of these topics is an example of narrowing it down. Explain to your child that if he or she wants to write about the people, the report will not include information about the mountains and rivers or the climate, unless of course they support the main ideas your child is writing about with regard to the people. For a shorter report, the topic can be narrowed down further. Suppose, for instance, you have selected the culture of a country. The report could focus on the food, holidays, religion, clothing, or any number of other aspects of a country's culture.

The other part of this standard focuses on the revision phase of writing. Explain to your child that writing involves several steps. The revision process is when a writer looks back at the draft to improve upon it. Revising the text involves reading it to make sure that the main idea is clearly stated; that there are facts, definitions, and details supporting the main idea; that the organization makes sense; and that there is no extraneous information. Writers should also look for vague or overused words during the revision process to see if they can find other options.

Once all revisions have taken place, the draft is ready to be edited. It is during the editing process that a writer checks to make sure that the grammar, spelling, and punctuation are correct.

A checklist like the one on the following page can help your child focus on identifying errors that need to be fixed.

To practice, have your child use the checklist to see how many errors he or she can find in the following paragraph. Have your child circle or underline any errors. Tell him or her to read through the article more than once to find all the errors.

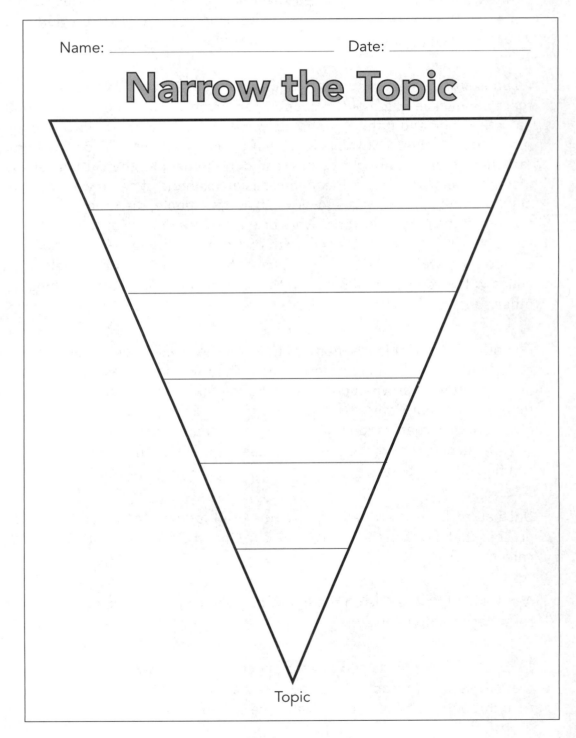

READ **France**

France is a country in Europe. There are many wonderfull things to see and do in France. In the capital city of paris is the Eiffel Tower. The Eiffel Tower was built over 150 years ago Another tourist spot is the Louvre. The Louvre is a museum with many famous paintings, including the Mona Lisa. The Mona Lisa is one of the most famousest paintings in the world.

There are other things to do in France besides visit paris. On the atlantic ocean and mediterranean sea, their are beautiful beaches. France also has mountains where you can ski or snowboard.

Name: _____   Date: _____

Narrow the Topic

Topic

Check-Up		
Focus/Ideas	Does the report have a clear topic?	
	Does the report stay on topic?	
Organization	Are the ideas presented in a way that makes sense?	
	Are ideas supported by facts, definitions, and details?	
Conventions	Does the writer use correct grammar?	
	Is the first word of each sentence capitalized? Are proper nouns (names of people and places) capitalized?	
	Is there a period at the end of each sentence? Are commas, quotation marks, question marks, and other punctuation marks used correctly?	
	Are all words spelled correctly?	

 **Answers**

France is a country in Europe. There are many wonderfull things to see and do in France. In the capital city of paris is the Eiffel Tower. The Eiffel Tower was built over 150 years ago_ Another tourist spot is the Louvre. The Louvre is a museum with many famous paintings, including the Mona Lisa. The Mona Lisa is one of the most famousest paintings in the world.

There are other things to do in France besides visit paris. On the atlantic ocean and mediterranean sea, their are beautiful beaches. France also has mountains where you can ski or snowboard.

? Quiz

Now that your child has found the errors, explain that the next step is to fix the errors. Have your child rewrite the paragraph so that it is error-free.

Answers

France is a country in Europe. There are many wonderful things to see and do in France. In the capital city of Paris is the Eiffel Tower. The Eiffel Tower was built over 150 years ago. Another tourist spot is the Louvre. The Louvre is a museum with many famous paintings, including the Mona Lisa. The Mona Lisa is one of the most famous paintings in the world.

There are other things to do in France besides visit Paris. On the Atlantic Ocean and Mediterranean Sea, there are beautiful beaches. France also has mountains where you can ski or snowboard.

The example provided gives a range of the types of things your child should look for in the revision and editing process. Point out that the report does a good job of narrowing down the topic (things to do in France). Main ideas of each paragraph are well defined, and there are facts and details to support the main ideas.

The errors relate to writing conventions. Point out the errors that have been made with capitalization (including the capitalization of words that do not need to be capitalized), punctuation, and spelling. Remind your child to look up the spelling of words that he or she is unsure of.

Extra practice

Play a game of hide and seek with your child in which you each try to "hide" one or more errors in a paragraph. The error can be related to grammar, capitalization, punctuation, or spelling. You can also try to hide a fact or detail that doesn't belong in the paragraph. Discuss why it doesn't belong.

The best way to practice revising and editing is to focus on the things your child is struggling with. If he or she has difficulty with spelling, for instance, focus on having him learn commonly used words and commonly confused words (such as *there/their/they're or to/two/too*). The Internet abounds with great worksheets on writing conventions.

OVERVIEW

For Grade 3, the Mathematics Common Core Standards focus on basic multiplication and division using whole numbers, with an emphasis on being able to visualize groups of objects to illustrate these principles. Similarly, the standards cover basic computation of area using visual models to show the number of square units being calculated. The standards also focus on the basic properties of fractions, using visual models to illustrate their meanings and relationships.

Listed below are the Mathematics Common Core Standards for Grade 3 that we have identified as "power standards." We consider these standards to be critical for your child's success. Each lesson in this section focuses on a single standard (or set of related standards) so that you and your child may practice that specific skill to achieve mastery. The applicable standards are divided into three categories: Operations & Algebraic Thinking; Number & Operations—Fractions; and Measurement & Data.

Operations & Algebraic Thinking

1. Multiplication and Division using Equal Groups

CCSS.Math.Content.3.OA.A.1: Interpret products of whole numbers, e.g., interpret 5×7 as the total number of objects in 5 groups of 7 objects each. For example, describe a context in which a total number of objects can be expressed as 5×7.

CCSS.Math.Content.3.OA.A.2: Interpret whole-number quotients of whole numbers, e.g., interpret $56 \div 8$ as the number of objects in each share when 56 objects are partitioned equally into 8 shares, or as a number of shares when 56 objects are partitioned into equal shares of 8 objects each. For example, describe a context in which a number of shares or a number of groups can be expressed as $56 \div 8$.

CCSS.Math.Content.3.OA.A.3: Use multiplication and division within 100 to solve word problems in situations involving equal groups, arrays, and measurement quantities, e.g., by using drawings and equations with a symbol for the unknown number to represent the problem.

2. Multiplication and Division using Arrays

CCSS.Math.Content.3.OA.A.3: Use multiplication and division within 100 to solve word problems in situations involving equal groups, arrays, and measurement quantities, e.g., by using drawings and equations with a symbol for the unknown number to represent the problem.

3. Multiplication and Division using Symbols for Unknown Numbers

CCSS.Math.Content.3.OA.A.3: Use multiplication and division within 100 to solve word problems in situations involving equal groups, arrays, and measurement quantities, e.g., by using drawings and equations with a symbol for the unknown number to represent the problem.

CCSS.Math.Content.3.OA.A.4: Determine the unknown whole number in a multiplication or division equation relating three whole numbers. For example, determine the unknown number that makes the equation true in each of the equations $8 \times ? = 48$, $5 = \_ \div 3$, $6 \times 6 = ?$

CCSS.Math.Content.3.OA.B.6: Understand division as an unknown-factor problem. For example, find $32 \div 8$ by finding the number that makes 32 when multiplied by 8.

4. Two-Step Problems

CCSS.Math.Content.3.OA.D.8: Solve two-step word problems using the four operations. Represent these problems using equations with a letter standing for the unknown quantity. Assess the reasonableness of answers using mental computation and estimation strategies including rounding. (This standard is limited to problems posed with whole numbers and having whole-number answers; students should know how to perform operations in the conventional order when there are no parentheses to specify a particular order.)

Measurement & Data

5. Multiplication and Area

CCSS.Math.Content.3.MD.C.7a: Find the area of a rectangle with whole-number side lengths by tiling it, and show that the area is the same as would be found by multiplying the side lengths.

CCSS.Math.Content.3.MD.C.7b: Multiply side lengths to find areas of rectangles with whole-number side lengths in the context of solving real world and mathematical problems, and represent whole-number products as rectangular areas in mathematical reasoning.

6. Adding Areas

CCSS.Math.Content.3.MD.C.7c: Use tiling to show in a concrete case that the area of a rectangle with whole-number side lengths a and $b + c$ is the sum of $a \times b$ and $a \times c$. Use area models to represent the distributive property in mathematical reasoning.

CCSS.Math.Content.3.MD.C.7d: Recognize area as additive. Find areas of rectilinear figures by decomposing them into non-overlapping rectangles and adding the areas of the non-overlapping parts, applying this technique to solve real world problems.

7. Measurement and Estimation

CCSS.Math.Content.3.MD.A.2: Measure and estimate liquid volumes and masses of objects using standard units of grams (g), kilograms (kg), and liters (l).1 Add, subtract, multiply, or divide to solve one-step word problems involving masses or volumes that are given in the same units, e.g., by using drawings (such as a beaker with a measurement scale) to represent the problem.2

Number & Operations—Fractions

8. Fraction Equivalence

CCSS.Math.Content.3.NF.A.3a: Understand two fractions as equivalent (equal) if they are the same size, or the same point on a number line.

CCSS.Math.Content.3.NF.A.3b: Recognize and generate simple equivalent fractions, e.g., 1/2 = 2/4, 4/6 = 2/3. Explain why the fractions are equivalent, e.g., by using a visual fraction model.

9. Comparing Fractions with Visual Models

CCSS.Math.Content.3.NF.A.3d: Compare two fractions with the same numerator or the same denominator by reasoning about their size. Recognize that comparisons are valid only when the two fractions refer to the same whole. Record the results of comparisons with the symbols >, =, or <, and justify the conclusions, e.g., by using a visual fraction model.

10. Fractions Greater than 1

CCSS.Math.Content.3.NF.A.3c: Express whole numbers as fractions, and recognize fractions that are equivalent to whole numbers. Examples: Express 3 in the form 3 = 3/1; recognize that 6/1 = 6; locate 4/4 and 1 at the same point of a number line diagram.

CCSS.Math.Content.3.NF.A.3b: Recognize and generate simple equivalent fractions, e.g., 1/2 = 2/4, 4/6 = 2/3. Explain why the fractions are equivalent, e.g., by using a visual fraction model.

THE STANDARD

3.OA.A.2: Interpret whole-number quotients of whole numbers, e.g., interpret 56 ÷ 8 as the number of objects in each share when 56 objects are partitioned equally into 8 shares, or as a number of shares when 56 objects are partitioned into equal shares of 8 objects each. For example, describe a context in which a number of shares or a number of groups can be expressed as 56 ÷ 8.

3.OA.A.3: Use multiplication and division within 100 to solve word problems in situations involving equal groups, arrays, and measurement quantities, e.g., by using drawings and equations with a symbol for the unknown number to represent the problem.

What does it mean?

The two major goals of third grade are understanding multiplication and division and understanding fractions. Students should be able to think of multiplication and division as equal groups, as area models and arrays, and as ways of finding unknown information. Because this topic is so important for third graders to master, it is covered in three lessons. This lesson focuses on multiplication and division using repeated addition and subtraction and by splitting or combining equal groups.

Try this together

To understand multiplication and division problems, help your child to identify these three parts: the number of groups, the number in each group, and the total. Visual models using circles and dots can help students to see and feel how these groups work.

In multiplication, you know the number of groups and the number in each group, and you need to find the total. In 5 × 2, you can think of there being 2 equal groups with 5 in each, or 5 equal groups with 2 in each. The total in both representations is 10, so 5 × 2 = 10.

    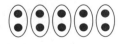

In division, you know the total and you know *either* the number of equal groups or the number in each equal group, but you need to find the other one. For example, the problem 10 ÷ 5 = 2 can ask the question "If you have 10 and divide them into 5 equal groups, how many are in each group?" It can also ask, "If you have 10 and make equal groups with 5 in each, how many groups will you have?" Your child can start by drawing groups or by drawing equal amounts for each group, and should practice using both methods.

In general, when students see word problems for math they should draw the actual objects in the word problems (like books, ducks, or children) but should instead stick to circles and dots. These representations are easy to draw and let students stay focused on the math. To provide a more hands-on experience, let students practice multiplication and division using small items like marbles, pebbles, or raisins to represent the objects and muffin tins or small cups to represent the groups.

These activities also lead to helping children break down word problems so they can solve them, and to develop their own math problems. As you practice with everyday story problems, help your child to identify the number of groups, the number in each group, and the total for each one. For example, using the problem above, you or your child could ask "If there are ten books and two friends each took an equal number of them, how many books did each friend take?" or "If there are ten children in a class and the teacher has them work n two equal groups, how many children are in each group?" Model with several examples so that your child can recognize the pattern. After creating a story, make sure that your child can draw a picture and write the math equation (10 ÷ 2 = 5).

? Quiz

1. Michael made 2 sandwiches every day for 7 days. How many sandwiches did he make? Draw a picture and write an equation to show your work. *First identify the number of groups, the number in each group, and the total, and use the information to draw a math picture. Then, write an equation that includes the answer.*

2. There are 16 levels left in Sandy's video game. If Sandy and her friend each play the same number of levels, then how many levels will they each play to finish the game? Draw a picture and write an equation to show your work. *First identify the number of groups, the number in each group, and the total, and use the information to draw a math picture. Then, write an equation that includes the answer.*

3. Mr. Yates has 15 pencils. His classroom has 5 desks. He draws a picture to answer a question about the pencils and the desks.

Which question is represented by Mr. Yates' picture?

A. *If Mr. Yates gives away 5 pencils, how many will he have left?*

B. *If Mr. Yates puts the same number of pencils on each desk, how many pencils will be on each desk?*

C. *If Mr. Yates puts 15 pencils on each desk, how many pencils will he need?*

D. *If Mr. Yates puts one more desk in the classroom, how many more pencils will he need so that each desk has the same number of pencils?*

4. Mr. O'Sullivan has 8 students in his class and he has each student do four assignments. Which can be used to find how many assignments there are in total?

A. $8 \div 4$ B. $8 \div 2$ C. 8×4 D. 8×2

5. Which question is answered with the division problem $25 \div 5$?

A. *Each jar has 25 candies. If there are 5 jars, how many candies are there?*

B. *If Sara practiced 5 math problems today and 25 math problems yesterday, how many math problems did she practice?*

C. *Aiden has 25 shirts. If he gives 5 shirts away, then how many shirts will he have left?*

D. *If a store had 25 fish and put an equal number in 5 tanks, then how many fish were in each tank?*

✓ Answers

1. Michael makes 2 sandwiches every day for 7 days. How many sandwiches did he make? Draw a picture and write an equation to show your work.

$2 \times 7 = 14$

The number of groups is 7 and the number in each group is 2. The total is missing, so this is a multiplication problem. Drawing a math picture shows that there are a total of 14 sandwiches. The first two questions are applications of the main standard. Even if your child can give the answer to the question without it, make sure to work with your child to draw a math picture and write the division problem or multiplication problem that represents the situation. This will help them in future, more complicated problems and standards.

2. There are 16 levels left in Sandy's video game. If Sandy and her friend each play the same number of levels, then how many levels will they each play to finish the game?

Draw a picture and write an equation to show your work.

 $16 \div 2 = 8$

The total is 16 and the number of groups is 2. The number in each group is missing, so this is a division problem. Students should start their math pictures by drawing two large circles, and then putting dots evenly into each circle until they reach 16 dots. The number of dots in each circle is 8, so $16 \div 2 = 8$.

3. Mr. Yates has 15 pencils. His classroom has 5 desks. He draws a picture to answer a question about the pencils and the desks.

Which question is represented by Mr. Yates' picture?

A. *If Mr. Yates gives away 5 pencils, how many will he have left?*

B. *If Mr. Yates puts the same number of pencils on each desk, how many pencils will be on each desk?*

C. *If Mr. Yates puts 15 pencils on each desk, how many pencils will he need?*

D. *If Mr. Yates puts one more desk in the classroom, how many more pencils will he need so that each desk has the same number of pencils?*

The correct answer is B.

Here, each desk is represented by a square and each has the same number of pencils drawn on it. It can be helpful to discuss how one would approach the questions from the other choices. For instance, A would be a subtraction problem. This question starts by giving students the total and the number of groups, and asks them to find the number in each group by identifying a word problem that uses division.

4. Mr. O'Sullivan has 8 students in his class and he has each student do four assignments. Which can be used to find how many assignments there are in total?

A. $8 \div 4$ B. $8 \div 2$ C. 8×4 D. 8×2

The correct answer is C.

The number of groups (8 students) and the number in each group (four assignments) are known and the total is missing, so this is a multiplication problem. Your child should recognize that when the number of groups (8 students) and the number in each group (4 assignments) is known, you are looking for the total so a multiplication problem is needed.

5. Which question is answered with the division problem $25 \div 5$?

A. *Each jar has 25 candies. If there are 5 jars, how many candies are there?*

B. *If Sara practiced 5 math problems today and 25 math problems yesterday, how many math problems did she practice?*

C. *Aiden has 25 shirts. If he gives 5 shirts away, then how many shirts will he have left?*

D. *If a store had 25 fish and put an equal number in 5 tanks, then how many fish were in each tank?*

The correct answer is D.

Each of the questions in the answer choices are different operations. Only D has a total of 25 being divided into 5 equal groups. Question 5 is the most difficult question because each answer choice uses the correct numbers in a different context. Your child should recognize that division problems start with a total and give the number of groups or the number in each group.

THE STANDARD

3.OA.A.3: Use multiplication and division within 100 to solve word problems in situations involving equal groups, arrays, and measurement quantities, e.g., by using drawings and equations with a symbol for the unknown number to represent the problem.

What does it mean?

A deep understanding of multiplication and division is important for success in third grade and beyond. The Common Core requires students to be able to show multiplication and division with objects and pictures in several ways. One of those is **arrays,** where objects are placed in equal rows and columns.

This array has 2 rows and 4 columns. It can show 2 groups of 4 each, or 4 groups of 2 each.

With this array, students can represent four math facts: $2 \times 4 = 8$, $4 \times 2 = 8$, $8 \div 2 = 4$, and $8 \div 4 = 2$.

Arrays give children another way of representing math visually, which makes them a powerful tool for solving word problems.

Try this together

Using the idea of equal groups, your child should be able to draw arrays to represent any multiplication or division problem up to $10 \times 10 = 100$. Talk with your child about ways to show 3×4. You can think of it as 3 groups of 4 objects each, by drawing an array that has 3 rows each with 4 objects. You can also think of it as 4 groups of 3 objects each, by drawing an array with 4 rows that each have 3 objects.

When working with your child, draw each of the possible correct arrays and verify that they are correct by counting. These arrays represent $3 \times 4 = 12$, so each should have a total of 12 circles.

For division, a single array can actually represent two different division problems depending on whether the groups are seen as rows or columns. Consider the array below which has a total of 20 circles.

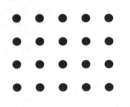

With your child, draw arrays like these and write the two division problems they could represent. If the rows are grouped together, the total of 20 has been divided into 4 equal groups. This represents 20 ÷ 4 = 5 because each of the groups has 5 objects in it.

Similarly, using the columns as groups would represent 20 ÷ 5 = 4 because each of the 5 columns has 4 objects in it.

? Quiz

1. Each of Cade's 5 friends brings 4 dollars to buy him a birthday present. How much money can his friends spend on his present? Draw an array and then write an equation to solve the problem.

2. Kelly has 14 animal crackers to give to her brother and her sister. If her brother and sister share equally, how many crackers will each of them get? Draw an array and then write an equation to solve the problem.

3. A quarter is equal to 5 nickels. Which picture represents the number of nickels equal to 6 quarters?

4. Henry and his mother are planting 42 flowers. They want to plant them in 6 equal rows. How many flowers can they plant in each row?

    A. 5   B. 6   C. 7   D. 8

5. Mary wants to use these stickers to decorate her folder.

    ☺ ☺ ☺ ☺

    ☺ ☺ ☺ ☺

    ☺ ☺ ☺ ☺

    ☺ ☺ ☺ ☺

    ☺ ☺ ☺ ☺

    Which expression can be used to find the total number of stickers?

    A. $5 \div 4$ B. $4 + 5$ C. $5 - 4$ D. 4×5

✓ Answers

1. Each of Cade's 5 friends brings 4 dollars to buy him a birthday present. How much money can his friends spend on his present? Draw an array and then write an equation to solve the problem.

    $$5 \times 4 = 20$$

    To represent this problem with an array, put 4 dots in each column to show that each friend brings $4. Make 5 columns to represent that there are 5 friends. In total, the friends bring $5 \times 4 = 20$ dollars.

2. Kelly has 14 animal crackers to give to her brother and her sister. If her brother and sister share equally, how many crackers will each of them get? Draw an array and then write an equation to solve the problem.

    $$14 \div 2 = 7$$

    Start with the idea of 14 total, and make a plan to create two equal rows. Your child should put a dot in the first row, then the second, and so on until all 14 are used up. There will be 7 in each row, so $14 \div 2 = 7$.

    These first two questions are designed to give your child practice in using arrays with word problems. Although it is possible to find the answer without an array, it is important that your child be able to use an array in each case. Work with them to sketch different possible arrays that may also be correct.

3. A quarter is equal to 5 nickels. Which picture represents the number of nickels equal to 6 quarters?

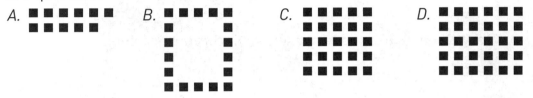

A.   B.   C.   D.

The correct answer is D.

Each quarter can be thought of as a group of 5 nickels, so the correct array will have 6 groups of 5. This is only the case for the array in D which has 6 columns with 5 objects in each one. Question 3 helps your child connect arrays that are already provided with the numbers given in a word problem. This is important as it makes your child approach the problem in a way they might normally. For example, if he or she typically uses an array with a certain shape and always uses rows for groups, a problem like this will make sure that there is recognition that other correct arrays are possible.

The incorrect answers represent common errors students may make. Answer choice A shows addition. B shows sides of a rectangle that are 5 units wide and 6 units tall, but which do not show equal objects in each row. Answer C shows a 5 × 5 array, which students may choose if they hurry and are not careful.

4. Henry and his mother are planting 42 flowers. They want to plant them in 6 equal rows. How many flowers can they plant in each row?

A. 6   B. 7   C. 8   D. 9

The correct answer is B.

This problem verbally describes an array with 42 total items divided into 6 equal rows, which your child may want to draw to answer the question. Division must be used to find the number in each row, and your child may already know the division fact 42 ÷ 6 = 7.

5. Mary wants to use the stickers shown below to decorate her folder.

☺ ☺ ☺ ☺
☺ ☺ ☺ ☺
☺ ☺ ☺ ☺
☺ ☺ ☺ ☺
☺ ☺ ☺ ☺

Which expression can be used to find the total number of stickers?

A. 5 ÷ 4   B. 4 + 5   C. 5 − 4   D. 4 × 5

The correct answer is D.

The keyword is total, so when the number of rows and the number in each row are known, multiplication can be used to find the total.

Students can also solve this problem by counting the number of stickers and then math facts to see if any of the answer choices are the same.

THE STANDARD

__3.OA.A.3:__ Use multiplication and division within 100 to solve word problems in situations involving equal groups, arrays, and measurement quantities, e.g., by using drawings and equations with a symbol for the unknown number to represent the problem.
__3.OA.A.4:__ Determine the unknown whole number in a multiplication or division equation relating three whole numbers. For example, determine the unknown number that makes the equation true in each of the equations $8 \times ? = 48$, $5 = \_ \div 3$, $6 \times 6 = ?$
__3.OA.B.6:__ Understand division as an unknown-factor problem. For example, find $32 \div 8$ by finding the number that makes 32 when multiplied by 8.

What does it mean?

This group of standards is focused on introducing algebraic reasoning and using basic equations or number sentences to solve problems. These techniques can also be applied to the word problems that have been covered in the last two lessons.

Try this together

The concept of equal groups in multiplication and division continue to be important when working with this group of standards. In lessons 1 and 2, students have practiced noticing three things: the number of groups, the number in each group, and the total. In all multiplication and division problems, two of these are known and the other one is not known or missing.

In math, we use symbols to represent values that are not known. These symbols can be letters like b or x, shapes like ∎ or ♥, or an empty box or question mark. For example, if there are 8 slices of pizza and they are shared equally by 4 people, the total and the number of groups are known, so you can write the division problem $8 \div 4$. The number in each group is not known, so you can use a symbol like p to show the number of pieces that each person gets: $8 \div 4 = p$.

Children often find it easier to start with empty boxes or question marks to represent the missing information, then move on to shapes, and then use letters. If your child is struggling with shapes or letters, switch back to empty boxes or question marks to reinforce the idea of the "missing" number that needs to be found.

Symbols can also be used to help students understand the relationship between multiplication and division. The problem $8 \div 4 = p$ can also be thought of as $4 \times p = 8$. Instead of figuring out a division problem, children can think of the number that is missing in the multiplication fact.

Children should be able to easily switch between all four facts in a "fact family," and notice that if they can find the value for p in one of them, it will work for all four equations.

$$8 \div 4 = p \quad 8 \div p = 4 \quad 4 \times p = 8 \quad p \times 4 = 8$$

Let's look at a few example questions that are similar to what a teacher may ask your child to do in class. As you review these questions, note that the standard is not focused only on "getting the right answer." Instead, your child may need to explain his or her reasoning through words or to select number sentences which reflect the correct kind of thinking needed to find the final answer.

? Quiz

1. Tony has 45 marbles and 5 jars. If he puts the same number of marbles in each jar, how many marbles will be in each jar? Write an equation that uses a □ to show the number of marbles in each jar. What is the □ equal to in your equation?

2. Rebecca gives her pet cat 3 treats each week. How many treats does she give her cat in 7 weeks? Write an equation that uses t to show the number of treats she gives her cat in 7 weeks. Then write a *different* equation that uses t to show the number of treats she gives her cat in 7 weeks. What is t equal to in your equations?

3. Chris makes 18 bracelets and gives an equal number to each of his 3 friends. Which number sentence could be used to find how many bracelets Chris gave each friend?
   A. $18 \times 3 = ?$ B. $18 \times ? = 6$ C. $18 \div ? = 6$ D. $18 \div 3 = ?$

4. What number could be used for the ♥ to make the number sentence true?
   $$4 \times ♥ = 24$$
   A. 4   B. 5   C. 6   D. 7

5. Which number sentence can be used to find the answer to $40 \div 8 = ☺$?
   A. $8 \times ☺ = 40$ B. $40 \div ☺ = 5$ C. $40 \times 8 = ☺$ D. $5 \times ☺ = 40$

✓ **Answers**

1. Tony has 45 marbles and 5 jars. If he puts the same number of marbles in each jar, how many marbles will be in each jar? Write an equation that uses a □ to show the number of marbles in each jar.

   Equation: $45 \div 5 = \square$

   What is the □ equal to in your equation? 9

   Your child should recognize that the total and the number of groups are known, so this is a division problem. The number in each group is missing, so the unknown value should be shown using a square. Students can think of filling in the square with the number 9 to make the equation true.

   Questions 1 and 2 both require your child to recognize the types of situations where multiplication and division can be used to answer questions and translate their understanding into an equation. To find the missing values, they can use math facts that are memorized, or draw math pictures or arrays.

2. Rebecca gives her pet cat 3 treats each week. How many treats does she give her cat in 7 weeks? Write an equation that uses *t* to show the number of treats she gives her cat in 7 weeks.

   Equation: $3 \times 7 = t$ or $7 \times 3 = t$

   Then write a different equation that uses t to show the number of treats she gives her cat in 7 weeks.

   Equation: $t \div 7 = 3$ or $t \div 3 = 7$ or a multiplication fact that was not used above

   What does t equal to in your equations? 21

   Children should notice that the number in each group (3 treats) and the number of groups (7 weeks) is known, but the missing information is the total. This can be shown with multiplication equal to an unknown: $3 \times 7 = t$. *To write a different equation, children can use other facts in the fact family to write a multiplication or division equation. To find the value of t, children can use math facts (memorizing that* $3 \times 7 = 21$*) or draw a math picture or array.*

3. Chris makes 18 bracelets and gives an equal number to each of his 3 friends. Which number sentence could be used to find how many bracelets Chris gave each friend?

   A. $18 \times 3 = ?$ B. $18 \times ? = 6$ C. $18 \div ? = 6$ D. $18 \div 3 = ?$

   The correct answer is D.

   Here, the question mark represents the unknown value. Since the problem is asking about dividing a total equally among groups, division is needed. The unknown amount is the result of the division problem, which is written as $18 \div 3 = ?$.

   However, an equation such as $3 \times ? = 18$ *would also be correct, because it shows the same relationship between the total, a known number of groups, and an unknown number in each group. This question asks students to identify how a symbol could be used to represent the unknown in a word problem. At this level, students are writing simple equations to represent the situation. This is built upon in later grades as students are introduced to algebra.*

4. What number could be used for the ♥ to make the number sentence true?

 4 × ♥ = 24

 A. 4   *B.* 5   *C.* 6   *D.* 7

 The correct answer is C.

 As an approach to this problem, have your child phrase a question in terms of the un-known value. For example "what number, when multiplied by 4, gives 24". The answer to this question is the value of the unknown which is 6. Your child may have memorized the multiplication fact 4 × 6 = 24, or may need to draw a math picture or array. This question introduces the idea in algebra of solving equations at a basic level. Instead of putting the missing information by itself on one side, it is shown within the multiplication problem.

5. Which number sentence can be used to find the answer to 40 ÷ 8 = ☺?

 A. 8 × ☺ = 40   *B.* 40 ÷ ☺ = 5   *C.* 40 × 8 = ☺   *D.* 5 × ☺ = 40

 The correct answer is A.

 This division problem represents 40 as the total. If the number 8 represents the number of groups, then the ☺ represents the number in each group. Answer choice A shows the same relationship as a multiplication equation, because the number of groups multiplied by the number in each group equals the total.

 To help your child see these relationships, use an 8 × 5 array to explore the connection be-tween this division problem and the related multiplication problem. While A, B, and D could all be represented by such an array, answer A uses ☺ as the unknown value. This question is testing whether students can see the relationship between division and multiplication. This is an important relationship in algebraic reasoning in later grades.

THE STANDARD

3.OA.D.8: Solve two-step word problems using the four operations. Represent these problems using equations with a letter standing for the unknown quantity. Assess the reasonableness of answers using mental computation and estimation strategies including rounding. (This standard is limited to problems posed with whole numbers and having whole-number answers; students should know how to perform operations in the conventional order when there are no parentheses to specify a particular order.)

What does it mean?

Under this standard, algebraic thinking and problem solving skills are expanded to more complex types of problems. Problems associated with this standard could use any of the four operations (addition, subtraction, multiplication, and division) and children will often need to use two different operations to find an answer. Finally, the concept of "reasonable-ness" is introduced as it relates to answers. This part of the standard is all about answering the question "does this final answer make sense?"

Try this together

Since problems may use any of the four operations, it is important that your child learn to recognize which type of operation makes sense given different types of situations. One way to help your child work on this is to help them identify key phrases using real life problems. For example, words like "less," "fewer," "take/give away," and "minus" all imply subtraction. You could ask questions such as "If you have 10 pieces of candy and give away 3, how would you figure out how many pieces you have left?" Remember that it is not the final answer that is most important here, but instead that the ideas associated with subtraction are recognized. Other key ideas are:

Addition: "more," "added to," "plus"
Example: If a teacher has twenty chairs and then gets three more, how many chairs will he have?
Multiplication: "per," "times," "each"
Example: If you want to give each of your three best friends two cards, how many cards will you need?
Division: "split into," "everly distributed," "divided into (groups)"
Example: If you want to share 30 stickers with 10 classmates and everyone gets the same number of stickers, how many stickers will each classmate get?

Once your child has become comfortable with recognizing the correct operation, you can begin to ask questions that require more than one operation and the final answer. If your child isn't sure where to start or gets an answer that is incorrect, help them see how to estimate the correct answer. For example, if you asked "What if we baked 3 cakes, cut each of them into 8 pieces, and then shared some with one of your friends? If we are left with 21 pieces of cake, how many pieces did your friend eat?", you should point out that you know the answer has to be smaller than 24, since that's how many pieces you started with and that if the friend only ate one piece there would be 23 left. So you know the answer must be bigger than 1. Finally, you can work with your child to draw a picture or write a number sentence (equation) to help find the right final answer. This question appears as #1 below.

Third graders should also understand the **order of operations** which states that multiplication and division should be performed before addition and subtraction. So to solve the equation $5 + 2 \times 8 =?$, start my multiplying 2×8 to get 16, and then add 5 to get 21. To show the addition or subtraction first, parentheses must be used: $(5 + 2) \times 8 = 7 \times 8 = 56$. Third graders are expected to write two-step equations, which they can do by writing the first equation, adding the next operation, and then checking to see whether or not they need parentheses.

It is also important to remember that addition and multiplication can be written in any order, but in subtraction and division the order is important. Often word problems will explain subtraction and division in the opposite order that they are written in math. For example, if Vijay gives 3 of his 6 markers to a friend, the subtraction problem is written $6 - 3$, not $3 - 6$.

❓ Quiz

1. Jonathan baked 3 cakes, cut each of them into 8 equal pieces, and then shared them with a friend. If he is left with 21 pieces of cake, how many pieces did his friend eat? Write an equation that represents the problem, and then solve it.

2. Angie made 8 red buttons and 6 green buttons. Then she shared them equally between herself and her brother. How many buttons did she keep? Write an equation that represents the problem, and then solve it.

3. Choose the number sentence that represents this problem:

Jacob wrote 5 pages each day for 4 days. If he needs to write 30 pages, how many more does he have to write?

A. $5 \times 4 + 30 = \square$ C. $30 - 5 \times 4 = \square$

B. $5 \times 4 - 30 = \square$ D. $30 + 2 \times 6 = \square$

4. Rachel bought some baseball cards and lost 3 of them. She put the cards that were left into 4 boxes with 5 baseball cards each. Which expression shows how many baseball cards she started with?

A. $5 + 4 - 3$ B. $5 \times 4 + 3$ C. $5 \times 4 - 3$ D. $5 + 4 + 3$

5. Fran drew the same number of pictures, p, every day for five days. The next day, she gave 10 pictures to her father. If she has 20 pictures, which equation represents the number of pictures she drew every day?

A. $p \times 5 - 10 = 20$ C. $20 \div 5 = p - 10$

B. $p - 10 \times 5 = 20$ D. $10 \times p - 5 = 20$

✓ Answers

1. Jonathan baked 3 cakes, cut each of them into 8 equal pieces, and then shared them with a friend. If he is left with 21 pieces of cake, how many pieces did his friend eat? Write an equation that represents the problem, and then solve it.

The correct equation is $3 \times 8 - 21 = 3$

First, children should use the clue "each" to recognize a multiplication situation. The total number of pieces is 3×8. Then, students should use the clue "left" to choose subtraction. Subtracting 21 from the total number of pieces will give the number that his friend ate. This can be written as $3 \times 8 - 21$. Because the multiplication step happens first, no parentheses are needed, though writing $(3 \times 8) - 21$ would also be correct.

To solve the equation, students should first multiply $3 \times 8 = 24$ and then subtract $24 - 21 = 3$.

The first two questions help your child recognize when problems require more than one step and which operations should be used for each step. Work with your child to decide what each step should be and how to write an equation with two steps to find the final answer.

If your child struggles with this, have them solve the problem first using two steps (such as $3 \times 8 = 24$, $24 - 21 = 3$) and then combine both steps into one equation. Point out that because 3×8 and 24 are the same amount, writing $3 \times 8 - 21$ is just like writing $24 - 21$.

2. Angie made 8 red buttons and 6 green buttons. Then she shared them equally between herself and her brother. Write an equation that represents the problem, and then solve it.

The correct equation is $(8 + 6) \div 2 = 7$

The clue "and" shows that addition must be used to find the total number of buttons that she starts with, so write 8 + 6. The clue "shared equally" represents division and Angie and her brother represent two groups. So the next step is to write (8 + 6) ÷ 2. Because division usually comes before addition, parentheses must be used to show that the addition comes first.

To solve the equation, start inside the parentheses and add 8 + 6 = 14. Then, move outside the parentheses and divide: 14 ÷ 2 = 7.

Writing 8 + 6 ÷ 2 without parentheses would be incorrect, because the first step would be to divide 6 ÷ 2 = 3, and the second step would be adding to get 8 + 3 = 11.

3. Choose the number sentence that represents this problem:

Jacob wrote 5 pages each day for 4 days. If he needs to write 30 pages, how many more does he have to write?

A. $5 \times 4 + 30 = \square$ C. $30 - 5 \times 4 = \square$

B. $5 \times 4 - 30 = \square$ D. $30 + 2 \times 6 = \square$

The correct answer is C.

The clue "each" represents multiplication. If he writes 5 pages each day for 4 days, he writes 5×4 pages. The clue "how many more" indicates subtraction. However, the number 30 is the total he needs and the number he has written already needs to be subtracted from this, so the 30 must come first in the math sentence: $30 - 5 \times 4$. The $\square$ represents the amount left. Because multiplication is preformed first, no parentheses are required.

4. Rachel bought some baseball cards and lost 3 of them. She put the cards that were left into 4 boxes with 5 baseball cards each. Which expression shows how many baseball cards she started with?

A. $5 + 4 - 3$ B. $5 \times 4 + 3$ C. $5 \times 4 - 3$ D. $5 + 4 + 3$

The correct answer is B.

Finding the answer here requires your child to work backwards and use clues in context. By finding the total number of baseball cards now, he can find the number of baseball cards there were at the beginning. Because each of the four boxes has five cards, there are a total of 4×5 cards left. Usually the clue "left" shows subtraction, but in this situation, the 3 cards were subtracted from a larger number that is unknown. To find this unknown number, 3 must be added to the amount left. Before the 3 cards were lost, there must have been $4 \times 5 + 3$ total cards.

In questions 3 and 4, the concept of a number sentence or equation is not as important as the idea of helping children see in which order operations should occur when finding an answer to a multiple step problem. This helps them avoid the common pitfall of simply trying different operations until they have a suitable answer. Knowing how to write the operations in the correct order will help them as they move into algebra in later grades. Question 4 especially focuses on thinking about the context as well as the clues on their own.

5. Fran drew the same number of pictures, p, every day for five days. The next day, she drew 10 more pictures. If she has 20 pictures, which equation represents the number of pictures she drew every day?

A. $5 \times p + 10 = 20$

C. $20 \div 5 = p + 10$

B. $p + 10 \times 5 = 20$

D. $10 \times p + 5 = 20$

The correct answer is A.

The clue "every day" represents multiplication. No matter what number p represents, if she draws the same number of pictures each day for 5 days, the total will be p × 5. The clue "gave" represents subtraction. Because she is subtracting 10 from a larger amount, the subtraction comes after the other amount: p × 5 − 10. The multiplication should be performed first, so no parentheses are needed. The clue "has" represents the = sign, so the amount that she has is equal to 20.

Note that in elementary school students are expected to write multi-step equations with unknowns in the calculations, but they are only expected to solve equations where the unknown is by itself on one side of the equal sign. Students will learn to solve equations like this one in middle school. This question helps students start to think of symbols, like p, as representing a number that can go anywhere in the problem instead of just "the answer." Thinking of symbols as stand-ins for numbers prepares students for success in algebra in middle and high school.

THE STANDARD

3.MD.C.7a: Find the area of a rectangle with whole-number side lengths by tiling it, and show that the area is the same as would be found by multiplying the side lengths.
3.MD.C.7b: Multiply side lengths to find areas of rectangles with whole-number side lengths in the context of solving real world and mathematical problems, and represent whole-number products as rectangular areas in mathematical reasoning.

What does it mean?

This pair of standards is focused on understanding what area is, and understanding why the area of a rectangle can be found by multiplying the side lengths.

Try this together

Area is a measure of the size of a flat surface. In third grade, students will find the area of rectangles in two ways. In the first approach, students begin with a unit square. This square has a length of 1 unit and a width of 1 unit. The area of the square is called "1 square unit."

1 unit

1 unit

Some example units for length and width measures are inches, feet, yards, miles, centimeters, meters, or kilometers. A unit square that is 1 inch long and 1 inch wide has an area of one square inch.

One way that your child can find the area of a rectangle is by placing unit squares on it without any gaps or overlaps and then counting the number of squares. This rectangle has 15 squares inside it that are each 1 centimeter by 1 centimeter, so its area is 15 square centimeters.

1 centimeter

1	2	3	4	5
6	7	8	9	10
11	12	13	14	15

1 centimeter

Using their knowledge of arrays, students should observe that the unit squares are arranged in rows and columns.

You can think of this rectangle as having 5 columns with 3 squares in each column, or 3 rows with 5 squares in each row. Whenever you have groups with the same number in each group, you can multiply or skip-count.

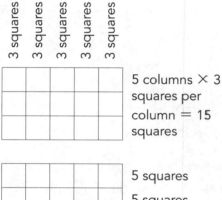

5 columns × 3 squares per column = 15 squares

5 squares
5 squares
5 squares

5 columns × 3 squares per column = 15 squares   3 rows × 5 squares per row = 15 squares

Once your child has a firm grasp on the concept of area using unit squares to count and using equal rows and columns of unit squares to multiply, you can move on to the general formula:

Area of a rectangle = length × width

Using this formula, your child can find the area of a rectangle without drawing each unit square. For example, this rectangle has an area of 4 feet × 8 feet = 32 square feet.

4 feet

8 feet

It is important that your child understands *why* this formula works, as well as being able to apply it in story problems. A good way to practice this idea with your child is to come up with real life scenarios and use graph paper to draw different possibilities. Asking the question "if we want to make a rectangular garden that is 20 square feet in area, what might it look like?" would give your child the chance to use the tiles or square units of the graph paper to represent different possible gardens. It is important when working with these ideas that your child pays attention to the units. Ask him or her to explain what one square unit of the graphing paper represents in the drawings.

With sketches such as these, students can also see the similarities between the square units in the rectangle and the arrays that they created for solving other multiplication problems.

As your child works with problems associated with these standards, have them create drawings, use the drawings they create to find the area by counting units, and find the area using multiplication. In order to be successful, they must see the connection between these ideas.

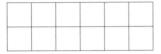 **Quiz**

1. What is the area of this rectangle?

   A. *2 square units*   B. *6 square units*
   C. *12 square units*   D. *16 square units*

2. Rashid wants to cover his rectangular kitchen with tiles. He uses 72 tiles that are each 1 foot long and 1 foot wide. Which measurements could describe his kitchen floor?
   A. *6 feet long and 8 feet wide*   B. *8 feet long and 9 feet wide*
   C. *9 feet long and 7 feet wide*   D. *10 feet long and 7 feet wide*

3. If the area of this rectangle is 40 square inches, then what is the length?

   4 inches

   ? inches

   A. *5 inches*   B. *10 inches*   C. *20 inches*   D. *36 inches*

4. Maya's backyard is a rectangle and measures 4 meters by 7 meters. What is the area of the back yard? Show two ways to find the area. Make sure to give the correct units.

5. On the grid below, draw two different rectangles that each have an area of 12 square units. Label the sides of your rectangles.

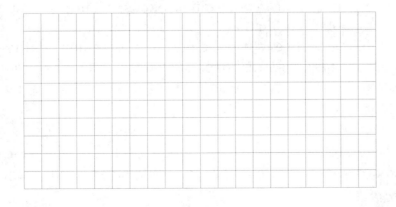

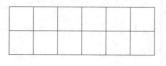 **Answers**

1. What is the area of this rectangle?

   A. 2 square units   B. 6 square units

   C. 12 square units   D. 16 square units

   The correct answer is C.

   This area can be found either by counting the number of unit squares that are within the rectangle or by multiplying the length (6 units) by the width (2 units). It is helpful to discuss both methods with your child.

   Question 1 checks that your child understands the concept of squares as a unit used in measuring area. After your child has answered this question, a useful activity is to go back and label the width and the height. He or she can then verify that the area is the same using multiplication, skip-counting, or counting individual squares.

2. Rashid wants to cover his rectangular kitchen with tiles. He uses 63 tiles that are each 1 foot long and 1 foot wide. Which measurements could describe his kitchen floor?

   A. 7 feet long and 9 feet wide   B. 8 feet long and 8 feet wide

   C. 9 feet long and 8 feet wide   D. 10 feet long and 7 feet wide

   The correct answer is A.

   Your child should use multiplication facts to check each answer choice. For A, $7 \times 9 = 63$, which is correct. To check, B is $8 \times 8 = 64$, C is $9 \times 8 = 72$, and D is $10 \times 8 = 80$. This question helps students transition from visual models where every unit square is shown to choosing their own method to solve the problem. Your child will likely choose to use multiplication facts to quickly check each of the answer choices, but he or she may want to check the answer by drawing a rectangle with unit squares and then skip-counting.

3. If the area of this rectangle is 40 square inches, then what is the length?

   4 inches

   ? inches

   A. 5 inches   B. 10 inches   C. 20 inches   D. 36 inches

   The correct answer is B.

   This question requires your child to work backwards. If the area is 40 square inches, then the length (?) times the width (4) must be equal to 40 inches. Students can write the equation $4 \times ? = 40$ and then use multiplication facts to determine that the ? represents the number 10. Students can also write the equation $40 \div 4 = ?$ to find that the missing length *is 10 inches.*

This is an advanced application of multiplication and area, and requires students to understand inverse operations (that multiplication and division are opposites). Students should be able to solve area problems when either the length, the width, or the area are unknown.

4. Maya's backyard is a rectangle and measures 4 meters by 7 meters. What is the area of the backyard? Show two ways to find the area. Make sure to give the correct units.

   The correct answer is 28 square meters.

   One way to find the area is by multiplying 4 × 7 = 28. Another way is drawing a rectangle with 4 rows that each contain 7 unit squares, and then counting them.

   Note that area is always measured in square units and because the length and width of the backyard are measured in meters, the area is measured in square meters.

   This question asks children to apply the concept of area to a word problem based on a real-life situation. Have your child draw a picture to represent the backyard on graph paper. When doing this, discuss the need to create a "key" for the area represented by a single square of the graph paper.

5. On the grid below, draw two different rectangles that each have an area of 12 square units. Label the sides of your rectangles.

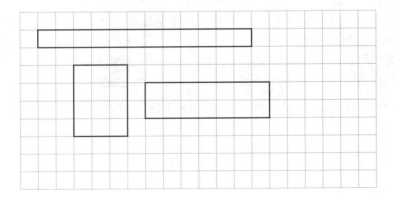

   There are three possible rectangles that have 12 unit squares inside: 12 × 1, 2 × 6, and 3 × 4 (though students are only asked to draw two of these). Be sure to have your child verify that each rectangle has an area of 12 units through counting and through multiplying the side lengths. This question is designed to help your child see that different rectangular regions may have the same area and that this area can be thought of in terms of how many tiles or square units are within the rectangle.

THE STANDARD

3.MD.C.7c: *Use tiling to show in a concrete case that the area of a rectangle with whole-number side lengths a and b + c is the sum of a × b and a × c. Use area models to represent the distributive property in mathematical reasoning.*

3.MD.C.7d: *Recognize area as additive. Find areas of rectilinear figures by decomposing them into non-overlapping rectangles and adding the areas of the non-overlapping parts, applying this technique to solve real world problems.*

What does it mean?

Students have already learned that the area of a rectangle is the product of its length and width. In these standards, they learn the important concept that the total area of two rectangles is the same as the areas of the rectangles added together. Standard 3.MD.C.7c lays the foundation for understanding the **distributive property**, which shows that the number outside the parentheses should be multiplied by each number inside the parentheses. For example, $5 \times (3 + 4) = 5 \times 3 + 5 \times 4$. Understanding the distributive property is critical for success in middle and high school math. Standard 3.MD.C.7d focuses on finding the area of irregular shapes by breaking them down into rectangles, a skill that students will use in middle school to find the areas of shapes like trapezoids and hexagons.

Try this together

Visualizing how rectangles and other figures can be broken down into smaller rectangles is the key to success with this standard. The area of this rectangle is 3 units × 4 units = 12 square units.

However, it is also possible to view the rectangle as two rectangles, a darker one that is 3 units × 3 units = 9 square units, and a lighter one that is 3 units × 1 units = 3 square units.

The total area of the whole rectangle is 9 units + 3 units = 12 square units. This is a visual way of showing the distributive property. We know that $3 \times (3 + 1) = 3 \times 4 = 12$ and we know that $3 \times 3 + 3 \times 1 = 9 + 3 = 12$. So, $3 \times (3 + 1) = 3 \times 3 + 3 \times 1$. The number outside the parentheses should be multiplied by each number inside the parentheses, and then the results should be added.

Your child should be able to recognize that any rectangle can be broken up in this way and that area of the large rectangle is the sum of the areas of the two smaller rectangles. Using graph paper, work with your child to take larger rectangles and break them into various small rectangles.

Expanding on this skill, your child will need to be comfortable breaking rectilinear figures (figures whose edges make right angles) into small rectangles and using the ideas above to find the area of the larger figure. As an example, consider the figure below.

The area of this figure can be found by breaking it up into rectangles two different ways:

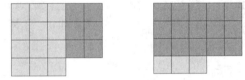

Using the figure on the left, the area of the lighter rectangle is 3 units × 4 units = 12 square units, and the area of the darker rectangle is 2 units × 3 units = 6 square units. The total area is 12 square units + 6 square units = 18 square units.

Using the figure on the right, the total area, in square units, is $(3 \times 5) + (1 \times 3) = 15 + 3 = 18$. Notice that no matter how the shape is divided into rectangles, the total area will be the same. When working with your child on problems with rectilinear figures, use graph paper and shading to see the different rectangles that make up any figure. There is not just one correct way to break up any given figure, so it is also useful to work with your child to find different ways to break up any figure and see that the area is the same.

? Quiz

1. Find the area of the figure below.

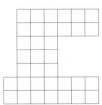

2. A rectangle is shown below.

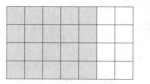

   Show the area of the rectangle in two ways by completing the equation.

   4 × (_____ + _____) = (_____ × _____) + (_____ × _____)

3. What is the area of the figure below?

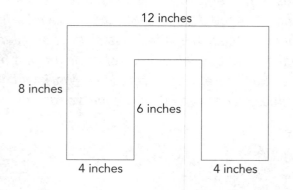

   A. *16 square inches*   C. *64 square inches*
   B. *40 square inches*   D. *72 square inches*

4. Which expression shows the correct area of the rectangle?

   A. (3 + 3) + (3 + 5)   C. (3 × 3) × (3 × 5)
   B. (3 × 3) + (3 × 5)   D. (3 + 3) × (3 + 5)

5. The sidewalk around Gerald's garden is shown below. If the sidewalk is 1 foot wide, then what is the area of the sidewalk?

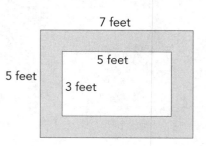

   A. *12 square feet*   B. *16 square feet*   C. *20 square feet*   D. *24 square feet*

✔ Answers

1. Find the area of the figure below.

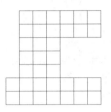

The correct answer is 36 square units.

There are several correct approaches to this problem. One method is to count the number of square units which make up the figure. Another is to break the figure into three or more smaller rectangles. The area of the figure is the sum of the areas of these smaller rectangles. This question is designed to help students see that the method of using the number of square units within a figure works even when the figure is not a rectangle. Work with your child to use this method, as well as breaking the given figure into rectangles and adding their areas.

2. A rectangle is shown below.

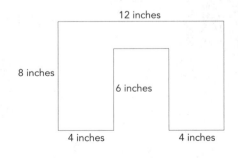

Show the area of the rectangle in two ways by completing the equation.

The answer is 4 × (_5_ + _2_) = (_4_ × _5_) + (_4_ × _2_)

The left side of the equation shows that multiplying the height of the rectangle, 4, by the width, 5 + 2 = 7, is one way to find the total area. The right side shows that adding the areas of the shaded section and unshaded sections results in the same total area. This equation overall shows the distributive property. This problem is designed to help children match the mathematical representation of the distributive property with a visual representation. The pattern seen here, of multiplying the number outside the parentheses by each number inside the parentheses, is one that they will see through college math and beyond, so it is important for them to become familiar with it now.

3. What is the area of the figure below?

12 inches

8 inches

6 inches

4 inches   4 inches

A. 16 square inches

B. 40 square inches

C. 64 square inches

D. 72 square inches

The correct answer is D.

The overall area of the figure can be found by breaking it into smaller rectangles in several different ways.

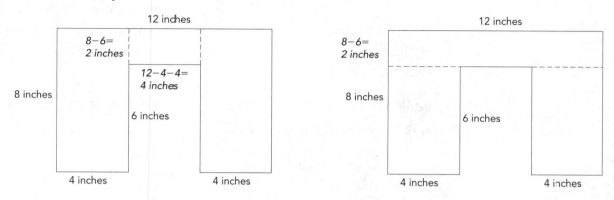

The figure on the left shows two rectangles that are each 4 inches by 8 inches. To find the dimensions of the third rectangle in the middle, use subtraction. The height of the whole figure is 8 inches and the inside is only 6 inches, so the part at the top must be 8 inches − 6 inches = 2 inches tall. To find the width of the middle rectangle, start with the whole width, 12 inches. Subtract 4 inches for each of the large rectangles. The width left is 12 − 4 − 4 = 4 inches. So the area of the whole shape is 8 × 4 + 8 × 4 + 2 × 4 = 32 + 32 + 8 = 72 square inches.

The figure on the right has two lower rectangles that are each 6 inches by 4 inches. The rectangle on the top is 12 inches wide. To find the height of the top rectangle, start with the height of the whole figure, 8 inches, and subtract 6 inches for the lower rectangles to get 8 inches − 6 inches = 2 inches. So the whole area is 6 × 4 + 6 × 4 + 12 × 2 = 24 + 24 + 24 = 72 square inches.

This problem moves students away from seeing each square to visualize area on a grid, and encourages them to find the area by multiplying. It is important for children to always draw the rectangles that they want to use on the figures so that they do not double-count some areas while skipping others.

This problem also gives students the opportunity to use addition and subtraction in finding missing dimensions. The length of the vertical line on the left is 8 inches, so the one on the right that is the same height must also be 8 inches. The height of the internal vertical line is only 6 inches, so the small rectangle at the top must have a height of 8 − 6 = 2 inches. In third grade, students should assume that all figures are accurately represented, so that if two lines look like they are equal, they are actually equal.

4. Which expression shows the correct area of the rectangle?

A. (3 + 3) + (3 + 5)

B. (3 × 3) + (3 × 5)

C. (3 × 3) × (3 × 5)

D. (3 + 3) × (3 + 5)

The correct answer is B.

The area of the whole rectangle equals the areas of both small rectangles added together. To find the area of each small rectangle, use multiplication. Their areas are 3 × 3 and 3 × 5, so the total area is (3 × 3) + (3 × 5). This question verifies that students understand how the area of two small rectangles relates to the area of the larger rectangle. With your child, verify that the total area you find is the same as the given expression by finding the total area several different ways.

5. The sidewalk around Gerald's garden is shown below. If the sidewalk is 1 foot wide, then what is the area of the sidewalk?

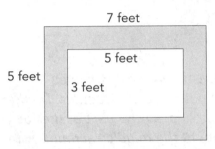

7 feet

5 feet

5 feet

3 feet

A. 12 square feet   B. 16 square feet   C. 20 square feet   D. 24 square feet

This problem can be solved in two ways. To solve it using addition, first divide the shape into rectangles. The distance across the sidewalk is always 1 foot, so use this number for the missing dimensions.

The area of the shape on the left is 5 × 1 + 5 × 1 + 5 × 1 + 5 × 1 = 5 + 5 + 5 + 5 = 20 square feet.

The area of the shape on the right is 7 × 1 + 7 × 1 + 3 × 1 + 3 × 1 = 7 + 7 + 3 + 3 = 20 square feet.

The second way to solve it uses subtraction. The area of the sidewalk can also be found by taking the area of the outside rectangle and subtracting the area of the garden inside: 5 × 7 − 3 × 5 = 35 − 15 = 20 square feet.

In this applied problem, students must use the given information to find the needed widths and lengths of the rectangles that make up the sidewalk. Work with your child to draw the smaller rectangles on the figure, or sketch the sidewalk on graph paper, and label each width and length.

THE STANDARD

3.MD.A.2: Measure and estimate liquid volumes and masses of objects using standard units of grams (g), kilograms (kg), and liters (l). Add, subtract, multiply, or divide to solve one-step word problems involving masses or volumes that are given in the same units, e.g., by using drawings (such as a beaker with a measurement scale) to represent the problem.

What does it mean?

This standard is focused on students' abilities to reason with measurement in common units and in their abilities to apply this reasoning to simple one step problems. The word problems associated with this standard will always use a single type of unit.

Try this together

The United States is one of only three countries in the world that use the Imperial or U.S. Customary System of measurement, which includes inches and pounds among its units of measure. Because of this, comfort with the metric system of measurement prepares children to be global citizens. Working with your child on concepts of measurement using real objects and measuring tools is important for success under this standard.

Students must learn to be comfortable estimating the volume or masses of everyday objects using grams, kilograms, and liters. This requires them to develop mental models of the relative "size" of these units of measure. To experience the mass of 1 gram, have your child hold a paperclip. A cell phone has a mass of about 100 grams, and a typical loaf of bread is about 500 grams. A one-liter water bottle both contains 1 liter of water by volume and has a mass of 1 kilogram. Of course, almost all products that you buy at the grocery store have their masses or volumes marked, so holding or pouring these objects can help your child experience the measurements.

Trying to estimate the weight of different everyday objects using the appropriate measure is good practice in expanding these baseline models. For example, a pot may be able to hold 4 liters, and this hypothesis can be tested by pouring in water from a 1-liter bottle until it is full. A drinking glass may be able to hold $\frac{1}{4}$ of a liter, which students can notice by pouring the water and then marking the sides of the 1-liter bottle to see the fraction that was used.

In third grade, students explore their first conversion of 1 kilogram = 1,000 grams. So if an object has a mass of 2,000 grams, this is equal to 2 kilograms. Discuss with your child that because grams are so tiny, you need a lot of them to make 1 big kilogram!

A second part of this standard is reading and understanding scales used in measurement. This would be similar to the scale used on measuring cups when cooking. When measuring ingredients for baking or other recipes, engage your child and have him assist you in measuring out the correct quantities for each ingredient.

? Quiz

1. Jamal's backpack has a mass of 9 kilograms when it is full. He takes out two books that each have a mass of 2 kilograms and one book that has a mass of 1 kilogram. What is the mass of his backpack after taking out the books?

2. Which has more mass: an object with a mass of 1,000 grams or an object with a mass of 2 kilograms?

3. Which amount is ABOUT the mass of a box of cereal?
   A. *3 grams*   B. *30 grams*   C. *300 grams*   D. *3 kilograms*

4. A scientist has the amount of water shown in the beaker below.

If she uses 3 liters, how much is left?
   A. *3 liters*   B. *4 liters*   C. *7 liters*   D. *10 liters*

5. Which amount is ABOUT the mass of a quarter?
   A. *6 grams*   B. *60 grams*   C. *600 grams*   D. *6 kilograms*

☑ Answers

1. Jamal's backpack has a mass of 9 kilograms when it is full. He takes out two books that each have a mass of 2 kilograms and one book that has a mass of 1 kilogram. What is the mass of his backpack after taking out the books?

   The correct answer is 4 kilograms.

   The clue "and" tells you to add the weights of the books 2 + 2 + 1 = 5 kilograms. The clue "takes out" is a clue to subtract this amount from 9 kilograms: 9 − 5 = 4 kilograms. This question asks students to use clues for choose operations in multi-step problems with measuring units. If your child struggles with this problem, you may want to review the lesson on Multi-Step Problems.

2. Which has more mass: an object with a mass of 1,000 grams or an object with a mass of 2 kilograms?

   The correct answer is the 2 kilogram object.

   Because 1,000 grams is equal to 1 kilogram, the 2 kilogram object is heavier than the 1,000 gram object. This question asks children to notice that amounts can only be compared when they use the same unit. Your child can convert 1,000 grams to 1 kilogram or 2 kilograms to 2,000 grams. Note that in third grade, children are only working with conversions with whole numbers of kilograms, not decimals or fractions.

3. Which amount is ABOUT the mass of a box of cereal?

   A. 3 grams   B. 30 grams   C. 300 grams   D. 3 kilograms

   The correct answer is C.

   A typical box of cereal has a mass of about 300 grams. For reference, 3 grams is about the mass of a few cereal pieces, 30 grams is about the mass of a metal cereal spoon, and 3 kilograms is a bit less than the mass of a gallon of milk. This question asks students to use their experiences with common masses to make an estimate. The best way to support children with questions like this is to have them lift, pour, and observe objects with common measures, and be alert to the masses and volumes written on the sides of products from the grocery store.

4. A scientist has the amount of water shown in the beaker below.

   If she uses 3 liters, how much is left?

   A. 3 liters   B. 4 liters   C. 7 liters   D. 10 liters

   The correct answer is B.

Using the given scale, the water line is halfway between the 6 liter and 8 liter marks, so there are 7 liters in the beaker. The clues "uses" and "is left" tell you to use subtraction: 7 liters − 3 liters = 4 liters.

This question addresses the ability of students to read measurements from common tools such as a beaker. Discuss with your child how to use the measurement lines to get a good estimate of the number of liters in this container. It is also worth discussing that not all beakers or measurement cups will use the same units. Because this is a two-step question, your child should notice that the answer is not the amount in the beaker, but the result of reading the beaker and then subtracting.

5. Which amount is ABOUT the mass of a quarter?

   A. 6 grams   B. 60 grams   C. 600 grams   D. 6 kilograms

   The correct answer is A.

   A quarter is about 6 grams, or about the mass of 6 paper clips. Like question 3, this question addresses the main skill behind this standard: the ability to reason with common measures of volume and mass. Each of these questions requires your child to have a good mental model of the relative size of these common measures and units.

THE STANDARD

3.NF.A.3a: Understand two fractions as equivalent (equal) if they are the same size, or the same point on a number line.

3.NF.A.3b: Recognize and generate simple equivalent fractions, e.g., $\frac{1}{2} = \frac{2}{4}$, $\frac{4}{6} = \frac{2}{3}$. Explain why the fractions are equivalent, e.g., by using a visual fraction model.

What does it mean?

Students should understand that fraction values can be represented in multiple ways. The Common Core places a strong emphasis on using bar models and number lines to represent the value of fractions, so that students can see and touch the fraction amounts in addition to thinking of them as numbers. These standards focus on equivalent (equal) fractions, which cover the same area on bar models and are placed in the same location on a number line.

In third grade, students are only expected to work with fractions that have denominators of 2, 3, 4, 6, and 8.

Try this together

Fractions represent a part of a whole. For example, pizzas are often cut into 8 slices, so if someone eats 4 slices, it can be said they ate $\frac{4}{8}$ of the pizza. The denominator, 8, shows the total number of parts, and the numerator, 4, shows the amount that is selected. The fraction $\frac{4}{8}$ of a pizza is the same as $\frac{1}{2}$ of a pizza. The fractions $\frac{4}{8}$ and $\frac{1}{2}$ are equivalent, and you can write $\frac{4}{8} = \frac{1}{2}$.

In the classroom, your child will use bar models to show fractions. This fraction shows a whole which is divided into 3 equal parts, and 4 of those equal parts are shaded.

This fraction shows a whole divided into 2 equal parts with one of the parts shaded. Both fraction bars have the same total size, and the shaded area is the same, so the fractions are equivalent.

Another model your child will see in the classroom is the number line. This number line shows the interval from 0 to 1. It is divided into 6 equal parts, so it shows fractions with a denominator of 6. If you start at 0 and move 2 parts to the left, you will reach the point $\frac{2}{6}$. The numerator is 2, because you have moved 2 parts.

Fractions are considered equivalent if they are in the same location on the number line. To show $\frac{2}{6}$ is equivalent to $\frac{1}{3}$, plot $\frac{1}{3}$ on the number line by dividing the number line into 3 equal parts and then start at 0 and move over 1 part. Notice that $\frac{2}{6}$ and $\frac{1}{3}$ are then in the same place on the number line.

With your child, pick equivalent fractions and use both models to show they are equivalent. In all cases, your discussion should focus on how the fraction represents the same "part" out of the "whole" and that the only change is how the "whole" is divided into pieces.

Note: In third grade, students are not expected to find equivalent fractions by multiplying or dividing the numerator and the denominator by the same number. This is a fourth grade skill. In third grade, students should rely on bar models and number lines to find equivalent fractions.

❓ Quiz

1. What is the location of point A on the number line below?

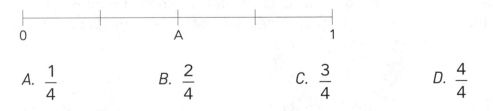

   A. $\frac{1}{4}$ B. $\frac{2}{4}$ C. $\frac{3}{4}$ D. $\frac{4}{4}$

2. What fraction represents the shaded area of the bar model?

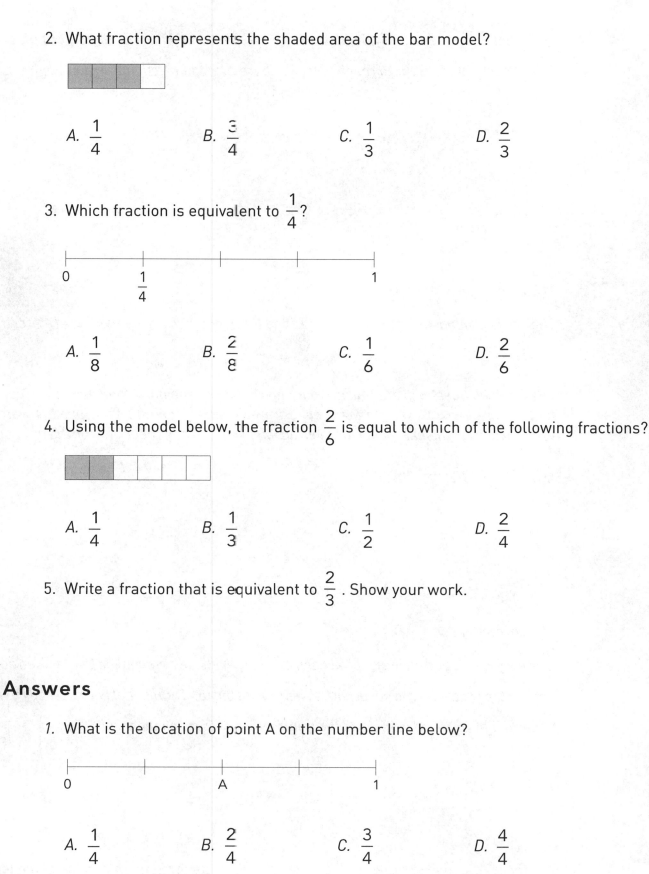

   A. $\dfrac{1}{4}$ B. $\dfrac{3}{4}$ C. $\dfrac{1}{3}$ D. $\dfrac{2}{3}$

3. Which fraction is equivalent to $\dfrac{1}{4}$?

   A. $\dfrac{1}{8}$ B. $\dfrac{2}{8}$ C. $\dfrac{1}{6}$ D. $\dfrac{2}{6}$

4. Using the model below, the fraction $\dfrac{2}{6}$ is equal to which of the following fractions?

   A. $\dfrac{1}{4}$ B. $\dfrac{1}{3}$ C. $\dfrac{1}{2}$ D. $\dfrac{2}{4}$

5. Write a fraction that is equivalent to $\dfrac{2}{3}$. Show your work.

✔ Answers

1. What is the location of point A on the number line below?

   A. $\dfrac{1}{4}$ B. $\dfrac{2}{4}$ C. $\dfrac{3}{4}$ D. $\dfrac{4}{4}$

The correct answer is B.

The number line is divided into four equal parts. Starting at point A, you must move 2 parts to the right to reach point A. Therefore, the fraction found at point A is $\frac{2}{4}$.

2. What fraction represents the shaded area of the bar model?

A. $\frac{1}{4}$ B. $\frac{3}{4}$ C. $\frac{1}{3}$ D. $\frac{2}{3}$

The correct answer is B.

The bar is divided into four equal pieces and three of those are shaded. Therefore, the fraction is $\frac{3}{4}$.

The first two questions are testing your child's understanding of the common visual models for fractions. A good exercise would be to draw the other model for each. In other words, have your child draw the bar model for the fraction in #1 and a number line for the fraction in #2.

3. Which fraction is equivalent to $\frac{1}{4}$?

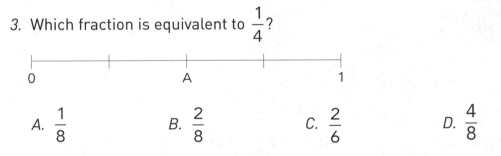

A. $\frac{1}{8}$ B. $\frac{2}{8}$ C. $\frac{2}{6}$ D. $\frac{4}{8}$

The correct answer is B.

One easy way to find equivalent fractions is to start with the number line that is given and divide each of the parts into two equal parts. Then, count the total number of parts (8) and the number of parts that you need to move to the right from zero to reach the point (2). So, $\frac{1}{4} = \frac{2}{8}$.

Another method is to draw each answer choice on its own line that is the same length as the line in the question. Start by using the denominator to divide the line into equal parts.

Then, count from the left to reach the number in the denominator. The line that has a point in the same location shows a fraction equal to $\frac{1}{4}$.

4. Using the model below, the fraction $\frac{2}{6}$ is equal to which of the following fractions?

A. $\frac{1}{4}$ B. $\frac{1}{3}$ C. $\frac{1}{2}$ D. $\frac{2}{4}$

The correct answer is B.

One way to find equivalent fractions is to look for parts that can be combined together to make larger equally-sized parts. Putting every two parts together to make 1 part results in the bar graph below, which shows 3 equal parts and 1 that is selected. So $\frac{2}{6} = \frac{1}{3}$.

5. Write a fraction that is equivalent to $\frac{2}{3}$. Show your work.

Sample correct answer: $\frac{4}{6}$. Work should be shown using a bar model or number line.

To generate equal fractions, start with a model. To draw a bar model, take a rectangle and divide it into 3 pieces, and then shade 2 of them to represent $\frac{2}{3}$. Then, divide each piece into two equal parts to create a bar divided into 6 pieces. Now, 4 of the parts are shaded, so $\frac{4}{6} = \frac{2}{3}$. The same procedure can be used on a number line.

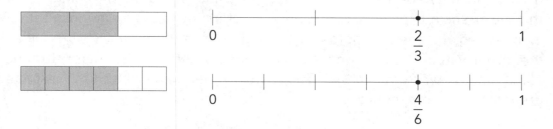

Questions 3, 4, and 5 ask your child to use the common technique of splitting parts into smaller parts that are also equal, or joining equal parts together to make larger parts that are also equal.

THE STANDARD

3.NF.A.3d: *Compare two fractions with the same numerator or the same denominator by reasoning about their size. Recognize that comparisons are valid only when the two fractions refer to the same whole. Record the results of comparisons with the symbols >, =, or <, and justify the conclusions, e.g., by using a visual fraction model.*

What does it mean?

This standard expands the basic standards associated with fractions and develops your child's skills in using mathematical comparison symbols correctly. Most of us are familiar with the idea that if the denominators are the same, the fraction with the smaller numerator is smaller because there are fewer parts selected: $\frac{1}{4} < \frac{3}{4}$. Children should also be familiar with the idea that if the numerators are the same, the fraction with the *smaller* denominator is *larger* because each of the pieces is larger: $\frac{2}{3} > \frac{2}{4}$ because thirds are larger than fourths, and you have the same number of them. As with other fraction problems, number lines and bar models are the main way of understanding the underlying properties of fractions. Only fractions with denominators of 2, 3, 4, 6, and 8 are studied at this level.

Try this together

To succeed with this standard, your child must be able to take the information from visual fraction models and translate it to a mathematical statement using <, >, and =. To do this, he or she must have a complete understanding of the meaning of these symbols. With inequalities, the easiest approach for children is to remember that the opening is towards the larger value (the alligator is always hungry and eats the biggest number). So, 3 < 4 could also be written as 4 > 3. These would then be read as "3 is less than 4" and "4 is greater than 3" respectively.

When working with the bar model, the concept of a fraction being larger or smaller can be understood by which fraction represents the larger or smaller shaded area. With the number line model, smaller numbers or values are always to the left of larger values.

In this standard, students are asked to specifically compare two types of fractions, those with the same numerators and those with the same denominators.

When fractions have the same denominators, all of the parts are the same size, and the fraction with more parts selected is larger.

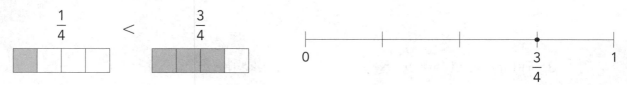

When fractions have the same numerators, each have the same number of parts selected. However, the fraction with the *larger* denominator has *smaller* parts so it is a *smaller* amount.

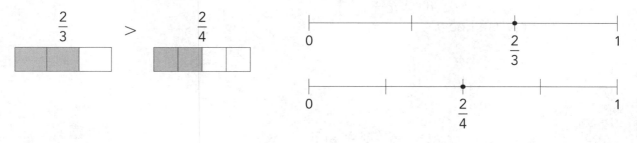

Your child should be familiar with these general rules for comparing fractions with the same numerator or same denominator. However, make sure to always use models before transferring to numbers—memorizing the rules without understanding how and why they work will not help your child in the long run.

Whichever model is used, help your child remember that the same "whole" must be used for each fraction being compared. Even though $\frac{3}{4}$ is larger than $\frac{1}{4}$ for the same whole, eating $\frac{3}{4}$ of an apple is less than eating $\frac{1}{4}$ of a watermelon.

❓ Quiz

1. Use the bar models below to compare $\frac{3}{6}$ and $\frac{3}{4}$ by writing an inequality.

2. Write an inequality that compares the fractions shown at points A and B on the number line.

3. Fill in the blanks with $<$, $>$, or $=$ to make the statements true.

a) $\dfrac{2}{6}$ _____ $\dfrac{4}{6}$ b) $\dfrac{2}{4}$ _____ $\dfrac{2}{3}$ c) $\dfrac{8}{8}$ _____ $\dfrac{6}{8}$

4. LaTasha read $\dfrac{1}{4}$ of a book. Rashid read $\dfrac{1}{3}$ of a different book. Who read more? Explain how you know.

5. Look at the fractions $\dfrac{2}{3}$, $\dfrac{1}{3}$, and $\dfrac{2}{4}$.

a) Draw the fractions on the number line below.

b) Write an inequality to compare them.

 Answers

1. Use the bar models below to compare $\dfrac{3}{6}$ and $\dfrac{3}{4}$ by writing an inequality.

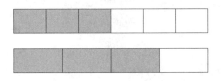

The correct answer is $\dfrac{3}{6} < \dfrac{3}{4}$.

Your child should count the total number of parts to find each denominator and count the number of shaded parts to find each numerator. The two fractions are $\frac{3}{6}$ and $\frac{3}{4}$. Your child should notice that the bar on top has less shaded area than the bar at the bottom, so $\frac{3}{6} < \frac{3}{4}$.

Use this model to point out that both have 3 parts shaded, but sixths are smaller than fourths because you need more sixths to make one whole.

2. Write an inequality that compares the fractions shown at points A and B on the number line.

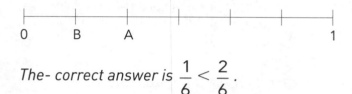

The correct answer is $\frac{1}{6} < \frac{2}{6}$.

To find the denominator of each fraction, count the number of equal spaces. It is important to count the spaces, not the lines! There are 6 equal spaces, so the line is divided into sixths. Point B is 1 space over from 0, and point A is 2 spaces over from 0, so the fractions are $\frac{1}{6}$ and $\frac{2}{6}$.

To compare them, notice that $\frac{1}{6}$ (or B) is to the left of $\frac{2}{6}$ (or A).

Questions 1 and 2 check your child's understanding of using bar models and number lines to name fractions and compare them. Your child should be able to explain to you verbally each step in finding the denominator and the numerator, and then comparing the fractions with each model.

3. Fill in the blanks with $<$, $>$, or $=$ to make the statements true.

a) $\frac{2}{6}$ ____ $\frac{4}{6}$ b) $\frac{2}{4}$ ____ $\frac{2}{3}$ c) $\frac{8}{8}$ ____ $\frac{6}{8}$

The correct answers are:
a) $<$ b) $<$ c) $>$

For part a, notice that the denominators are the same, so the parts are the same size. The numerator 2 is smaller than 4, so $\frac{2}{6} < \frac{4}{6}$. For part b, the numerators are the same, so the fraction with the larger denominator, 4, has smaller parts. Thus, $\frac{2}{4} < \frac{2}{3}$. For part c, the denominators are the same, so the parts are the same size. The numerator 8 is larger than

6, so $\dfrac{8}{8} > \dfrac{6}{8}$. Notice that $\dfrac{8}{8}$ is the same as 1 whole.

These inequalities should all be reinforced using bar models or number lines. Encourage your child to represent them with both models.

Question 3 addresses the basic rules of comparisons for the same numerators or same denominators. Be sure that your child understands the general rules and sketches pictures to help him visualize the comparison. Encourage him to try both the bar model and the number line model.

4. LaTasha read $\dfrac{1}{4}$ of a book. Rashid read $\dfrac{1}{3}$ of a different book. Who read more? Explain how you know.

The correct answer is that these fractions cannot be compared.

Although the fraction $\dfrac{1}{4}$ is less than $\dfrac{1}{3}$ when they are part of the same whole, we have no way of knowing who read more because the two books are different. LaTasha might have read $\dfrac{1}{4}$ of a very long book while Rashid read $\dfrac{1}{3}$ of a very short book, in which case LaTasha would have read more. This question addresses the idea that the whole must be the same for fractions to be compared. If your child struggles with this question, it may help to compare pages from actual books.

5. Look at the fractions $\dfrac{2}{3}$, $\dfrac{1}{3}$, and $\dfrac{2}{4}$.

a) Draw the fractions on the number line below.

b) Write an inequality to compare them.
The correct answers are:

a)

b) $\dfrac{1}{3} < \dfrac{2}{4} < \dfrac{2}{3}$

To draw the points on the number line, your child should first draw equally spaced lines to divide it into 3 equal parts and count from 0 to label $\frac{1}{3}$ and $\frac{2}{3}$. She should then divide it into 4 equal parts and count 2 of them to label $\frac{2}{4}$.

To write an inequality, your child should write the fractions on the number line from left to right and use the $<$ sign.

Question 5 requires your child to both draw a free-hand number line (an important skill in comparison) and to write an inequality that involves three numbers. Your child should be able to recognize that $\frac{1}{3} < \frac{2}{3}$ because they have the same denominator, and that $\frac{2}{4} < \frac{2}{3}$ because they have the same numerator. Comparing $\frac{1}{3}$ and $\frac{2}{4}$ can, at this point, only be done by using a visual model.

THE STANDARD

3.NF.A.3c: Express whole numbers as fractions, and recognize fractions that are equivalent to whole numbers. Examples: Express 3 in the form $3 = \frac{3}{1}$; recognize that $\frac{6}{1} = 6$; locate $\frac{4}{4}$ and 1 at the same point of a number line diagram.

3.NF.A.3b: Recognize and generate simple equivalent fractions, e.g., $\frac{1}{2} = \frac{2}{4}, \frac{4}{4} = \frac{2}{3}$. Explain why the fractions are equivalent, e.g., by using a visual fraction model.

What does it mean?

Whole numbers can also be represented by fractions, and this standard addresses that quality for fractions with denominators of 1, 2, 4, 6, and 8. With the number line model, it is possible to use the same general ideas as those used with other fractions standards to show that for any nonzero number a, $\frac{a}{a} = 1$. This is then expanded to consider fractions such as $\frac{12}{4}$ or $\frac{8}{2}$. In third grade, students will also see fractions that are greater than 1, but are not equal to whole numbers, such as $\frac{3}{2}$, which is the same as $1\frac{1}{2}$.

Try this together

Conceptually, this standard can be difficult for students as they have mostly encountered fractions in which the numerator is smaller than the denominator. In order to be successful, however, students must be able to think of whole numbers and their equivalent fractions.

For example, if a carrot were cut into 4 pieces, then 2 pieces would represent $\frac{2}{4}$. Four pieces would represent the whole carrot, so $\frac{4}{4} = 1$. Further, if there are two carrots that are the same size and each of them is divided into 4 equal parts, then there are 8 fourths which together make two carrots, so $\frac{8}{4} = 2$.

The amount $\frac{8}{4}$ can be represented with bar models by drawing two wholes and dividing *each* of them into 4 equal parts because 4 is the numerator. Because the denominator is 8, there must be 8 parts shaded. The result is 2 wholes.

On a number line, *each* space between whole numbers represents a whole. This number line shows one whole between 0 and 1 and another whole between 1 and 2. To show $\frac{8}{4}$, *each* whole is separated into 4 equal parts, and then 8 of those parts are counted, starting from 0 and moving left.

Your child will also encounter fractions which are greater than 1, but are not equal to whole numbers. These numbers can be written as **improper fractions** which have a numerator that is larger than the denominator, or as **mixed numbers** which have a whole number and a fraction. For example, the improper fraction $\frac{5}{4}$ is equivalent to 1 whole and one more fourth, or the mixed number $1\frac{1}{4}$. Here is $1\frac{1}{4}$ shown on a number line and with fraction models:

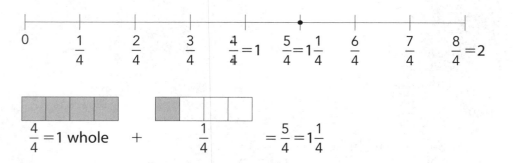

As with previous fraction standards, work with your child to create visual and other conceptual models to understand the magnitude of these fractions. These models don't just help solidify their understanding of fractions but also help prepare them for future courses where number lines and fractions are common.

? Quiz

1. Draw models:

   a) Use a number line to show that $\frac{4}{4} = 1$.

   0

b) Use a bar model to show that $\dfrac{6}{2} = 3$.

2. Express this fraction as a mixed number and an improper fraction:

3. Which of the following fractions is **not** equal to 2?

   A. $\dfrac{2}{1}$ B. $\dfrac{2}{2}$ C. $\dfrac{4}{2}$ D. $\dfrac{6}{3}$

4. The fraction $\dfrac{10}{4}$ is equal to which of the following numbers?

   A. $1\dfrac{1}{4}$ B. $1\dfrac{2}{4}$ C. $2\dfrac{2}{4}$ D. $10\dfrac{1}{4}$

5. The fraction $\dfrac{2}{2}$ is equivalent to which of the following numbers?

   A. 1 B. 2 C. 3 D. 4

☑ Answers

1. Draw models:

a) Use a number line to show that $\dfrac{4}{4} = 1$.

b) Use a bar model to show that $\dfrac{6}{2} = 3$.

The correct answers are:

a)

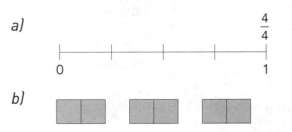

b)

For part a, begin with 1 whole, and divide it into 4 equal parts to show fourths. Counting 4 of them reaches the same point as 1 whole, so $\frac{4}{4} = 1$.

For part b, begin with 3 wholes and divide each of them into 2 equal pieces. Then, shade 6 halves to show that $\frac{6}{2} = 3$.

In this question, your child must take a given equivalence and show it visually. Once the problem is completed, it would be useful for you to discuss the other fractions on the number line and fractions which may be equivalent to them.

2. Express this fraction as a mixed number and an improper fraction:

The correct answer is $1\frac{5}{6}$ and $\frac{11}{6}$.

To find the mixed number, your child should notice that there is 1 whole and $\frac{5}{6}$ left over. To find the improper fraction, your child should notice that each whole is divided into 6 equal parts, and that a total of 11 of them are shaded.

This question gives asks students to work with fractions greater than 1 using a bar model. Your child should always recognize that when a whole bar is filled, this is equal to 1, and that the parts left over are represented by a fraction. Point out that both wholes are divided into 6 equal parts, which is why the denominator is 6.

3. Which of the following fractions is **not** equal to 2?

A. $\frac{2}{1}$ B. $\frac{2}{2}$ C. $\frac{4}{2}$ D. $\frac{6}{3}$

The correct answer is B.

To solve this problem, encourage your child to draw a number line from 0 to 2, or to create a bar model showing two wholes. Then, have your child test each answer by dividing each of the wholes into the number of parts shown in the denominator.

As a general rule, any fraction with 1 in the denominator is equal to the number in the numerator, so $\frac{2}{1} = 2$. Any fraction with the same numerator and denominator is equal to 1, so $\frac{2}{2} = 1$. If your child knows these rules, he should be able to identify B as the correct answer because it equals 1 without testing the others.

Question 3 requires your child to use the way the answer choices are presented in deciding *how to answer the question. By being given the whole number first, your child may choose to start by drawing a number line or bar model that shows 2 wholes, and then subdivide it. Work with your child to identify each of the answer choices on the model and discuss whether or not they are equivalent to 2.*

This question also addresses two rules in fractions, that $\dfrac{x}{1} = x$ and $\dfrac{z}{z} = 1$. Encourage your child to see these as general rules, and also to try the other fractions in the question.

4. The fraction $\dfrac{10}{4}$ is equal to which of the following numbers?

   A. $1\dfrac{1}{4}$ B. $1\dfrac{2}{4}$ C. $2\dfrac{2}{4}$ D. $10\dfrac{1}{4}$

The correct answer is C.

This problem can be addressed by starting with a number line or a bar model, and continuing to extend the number line until 10 fourths can be drawn, or adding more whole bars until 10 fourths are shown. The first whole will use 4 fourths, the second whole will use 4 more fourths (for a total of 8) and there will be two left over. The equivalent mixed number is $2\dfrac{2}{4}$.

This question looks at an improper fraction which is not only greater than 1, but is actually greater than 2. Remind your child when drawing models that each whole should be divided into the same number of parts (in this case 4), and that he should keep adding more wholes until there are enough parts.

5. The fraction $\dfrac{2}{2}$ is equivalent to which of the following numbers?

   A. 1   B. 2   C. 3   D. 4

The correct answer is A.

The whole is divided into 2 pieces. Using a bar model, if 2 parts are shaded, it can be seen that the entire whole is shaded. Therefore, $\dfrac{2}{2} = 1$.

This question again highlights the rule that for any nonzero number a, a/a = 1. You and your child should draw many different models using different values of a to solidify this rule and the rule $\dfrac{a}{1} = a$.

ENGLISH LANGUAGE ARTS POST-TEST

The following questions are intended to assess your child's reading skills. As with the pre-test, there are a variety of question types at various levels of cognition. These are typical of the types of questions that your third grader might experience in the classroom, as homework, and in assessment situations. These items are **not** designed to replicate standardized tests used to assess a child's reading level or a school's progress in helping the child achieve grade level.

A grid at the end provides the main Common Core standard assessed, as well as a brief explanation of the correct answers. This is intended to help you consider how your child is doing in reading and writing after you have presented the lessons in this book. Keep in mind, however, that building reading and writing skills is an ongoing process. The best way to build these skills is to continue to read and write. If the post-test identifies areas in which your child needs improvement, review the strategies in the lessons and continue to focus on these areas when you read with your child.

Some of the questions are based on stories or other reading passages. Read the passage carefully. If you don't know the answer to a question, look back at the passage to see if you can find it.

For each section, read the passage and then answer the questions that follow.

 Untitled

Bella skipped into the kitchen, wiping sleep from her eyes. "Can we go to the park today?" she asked.

"I don't think so," said her mom, looking out the kitchen window. "It looks like it's going to rain."

Bella frowned and looked down into the oatmeal her mother put in front of her. "But I told Alexandra that we could meet her there."

"Maybe Alexandra can come here today," her mom suggested.

To Bella that didn't sound like a lot of fun. It had been a long time since she had gotten any new toys or arts and crafts, and Alexandra did not like board games.

"If we're going to have guests, there's some work to do in the living room," said Bella's dad.

"Can you help me please, Bella?"

Bella didn't want to clean the living room, but her dad's tone didn't leave her much choice.

"Go on," coaxed Bella's mom. "It will just take a minute. You can finish your oatmeal afterward. It's too hot to eat anyway."

Bella slid off her chair and walked slowly into the living room, where her father was waiting for her.

"Surprise!" yelled her father. Bella's eyes opened wide. There was a big cardboard playhouse in the middle of the room. Her father stood beaming, with a stack of markers and stickers in his hand. "It needs some work," he said. "Maybe Alexandra can help you out."

Bella nodded. She didn't want to go to the park anymore.

1. Which word best describes how Bella feels when she learns it is supposed to rain?

   A. angry   B. bored   C. disappointed   D. surprised

2. What details in the text helped you answer question #1?

   _____

   _____

3. Why does Bella's father ask her to go into the living room?

   A. He wants to ask her to call Alexandra.

   B. He wants her to help clean up the room.

   C. He wants to give her markers and stickers.

   D. He wants to surprise her with a new playhouse.

4. Read the sentence from the story.

   "Go on," coaxed Bella's mom. "It will just take a minute."

   Using context clues, what does *coaxed* mean?

   A. argued   B. cheered   C. encouraged   D. yelled

5. Which would be the **best** title for this story?

   A. Bella and Alexandra   C. Rainy Weather

   B. A Surprise for Bella   D. A Trip to the Park

6. Why doesn't Bella want to go to the park at the end of the story?

   _____

   _____

 The First Flight

If you look in the sky today, you would not be surprised to see a plane soar by. But it took many years for people to figure out how to make planes as safe as they are today.

Although many people had dreamed of flying, it was Orville and Wilbur Wright who made the dream come true. The Wright brothers owned a shop in Dayton, Ohio, where they made and repaired bicycles. They used their understanding of how bicycles work to figure out how a plane might work. They had seen how important balance was to riding a bicycle. The Wright brothers thought that balance would also be important in flying a plane.

The Wright brothers also studied how to steer the airplane. They set up experiments in their bicycle shop to try different wings and propellers, which are used to move the plane forward. Then they spent several years testing gliders, which have wings but no engine. They used what they learned to figure out how to attach the engine to something that would fly.

On December 17, 1903, the Wright brothers succeeded in their mission. In a big field in Kitty Hawk, North Carolina, Orville Wright steered a plane off the ground. It stayed in the air for only twelve seconds, but that was long enough to prove that flying was possible.

7. Read the sentence from the passage.

"If you look in the sky today, you would not be surprised to see an airplane soar by."

Using context clues, what does *soar* mean?

_____

_____

8. Put the following events in order.

____ *The Wright brothers fly a plane.*

____ *The Wright brothers test gliders.*

____ *The Wright brothers open a bicycle shop.*

____ *The Wright brothers experiment with propellers.*

9. Write a paragraph describing how Orville and Wilbur Wright figured out how an airplane works. What personality traits did they have that helped them to be successful? Write your paragraph in your own words. Use correct grammar, punctuation, and spelling.

_____

_____

 ## Going Green

"Going green" is a term that is used to describe the things people do to protect the world around us. There are three basic parts of going green, sometimes called the "three Rs": reduce, reuse, and recycle.

Reducing means using less. You can reduce your use of water, electricity, and other natural resources. You can take shorter showers or turn off the water when you are brushing your teeth. Turning off the television and other appliances is also a good way to reduce the use of electricity.

Reusing is another way you can help the environment. Reusing things means to find new uses for something rather than tossing it into the trash. An old shirt can become a dust rag, or an old toothbrush can be used to clean the grout in the bathroom. Taking your own bag to the grocery store is a way to both reuse and reduce.

The final "R" is recycling. Recycling converts old products into new ones. People cannot do their own recycling because it requires special machines. In some communities, there is a recycling truck that picks up paper, cardboard, glass, plastic, and other recyclable materials at the curb. In other places, people need to take these materials to a recycling center. Glass bottles can be crushed, melted, and made into new ones. Plastic also can be melted. In addition to new plastic containers or parts, recycled plastic is sometimes woven into fiber that is used to make rugs or carpets. Fleece is one of the most common fabrics made from plastic. Remember those plastic grocery bags you put in the recycling bin? They may come back as a fleece jacket!

10. Which of the following is an example of reusing something?
    A. *A soda bottle is made into fleece.*
    B. *Water is taken directly from a stream.*
    C. *A milk carton is used to water the plants.*
    D. *The toaster is unplugged when not being used.*

11. Which sentence tells the main idea of the last paragraph?
    A. *The final "R" is recycling.*
    B. *Recycling converts old products into new ones.*
    C. *Glass bottles can be crushed, melted, and made into new ones.*
    D. *Fleece is one of the most common fabrics made from plastic.*

12. Read the sentence from the passage.

    "Recycling converts old products into new ones."

    Using context clues, what does *convert* mean?
    A. *change*
    B. *fix*
    C. *give away*
    D. *throw out*

13. Read the sentence from the passage.

    "Fleece is one of the most common fabrics made from plastic."

    Which word in this sentence best helps you know what *fabric* means?
    A. *fleece*   B. *one*   C. *common*   D. *plastic*

14. What is the goal of "Going Green"? What does the author want readers to do? Use details from the text to support your answer. Use correct grammar, punctuation, and spelling.

    _____

    _____

    _____

 ## The Treasure in the Field

Once there was a farmer who worked hard in his field to grow crops. His family used some of these crops for food, and sold the rest to buy other things they needed. He had only one son, and it was always his desire that his son would one day take charge of the farm. Then the farmer would finally have a chance to rest his weary bones.

The farmer's son, however, was not interested in farming. Working the farm meant spending long days outside in the heat and the cold, toiling away until the sun went down. Instead, the son spent his time trying to gain money through all sorts of other ways that did not involve hard work. These plans never amounted to much, and the son always ended up even poorer than he was when he started.

One spring, just before it was time to plant the crops, the farmer became sick. He could not go out and work the field, so he asked his son to do it instead. The son replied, "Father, I'm working on so many other schemes right now that I just don't have the time."

The farmer was saddened by his son's answer. If no one planted the crops, the farmer and his family would have no food, and no money. So the farmer came up with a clever plan to trick his son. "My son," he said, "I have just remembered that there is a priceless family treasure buried somewhere in our field. If only we could find it, our problems would be solved."

The son's ears perked up. "Treasure? Where is this treasure?"

"I only know that it is buried in our field," the farmer said. "If someone dug up the soil, they might be able to find it."

Upon hearing this, the son went outside and began digging up the field. He began at one end and made even rows across the field, searching every bit of it for the treasure. When he came back inside, he was exhausted. "Father," he said between his breaths, "I looked everywhere in the field, and I cannot find a treasure."

"Oh," the farmer said. "I just remembered that it is buried deep under the soil. If you plant seeds in the soil you dug up, then the roots will grow down and find the treasure. The plants that grow above the treasure will be golden, and you will know where the treasure is."

The next day the son worked hard to plant seeds all across the field, and made sure they were well covered in soil. After a few months, the farmer finally recovered from his sickness, and the seeds in the field had grown into tall stalks.

"Father," the son said. "I still cannot figure out where the treasure is."

"Why not?" the farmer asked.

"Every stalk in the field is golden in color," said the son.

"Ah," said the farmer. "Then there is your answer. The treasure is this beautiful crop that will feed us and bring us money for the year. You did not want to work the field until you thought it held secret treasure. And now you know the truth: every year the field holds all the treasure we need, if only we're willing to work for it."

15. Which word best describes the farmer?

 A. hardworking   B. lazy   C. angry   D. young

16. What detail from the story supports your answer?

_____

_____

17. Describe the farmer's son. How is he different from his father? Use details from the story.

_____

_____

18. How does the farmer convince his son to work the field?

_____

_____

19. Fables often have morals, or lessons they are meant to teach. Which sentence from the story best sums up the lesson the story is trying to teach?

_____

_____

 Read the story about Max. Then answer the questions that follow.

> Max opened the front door and quietly entered his house. He couldn't believe that his mom wasn't at the door to greet him, today of all days! He suspected that she was upstairs trying to get his baby sister to nap.
>
> As Max hung up his backpack, he noticed that something was out of place. It took a few seconds for Max to notice what it was. The old beat-up tennis racket that usually hung on the hook next to the garage door had been replaced with the one he had been eying at the store last month. His parents had not forgotten his birthday after all!

20. Which best describes how Max feels when he walks in the door of his house?
    A. disappointed   B. happy   C. surprised   D. tired

21. Read the sentence from the story.
    "He couldn't believe that his mom wasn't at the door to greet him, today of all days!"
    Why is Max surprised that she is not meeting him "today of all days"?
    A. It is his birthday.   C. He has had a bad day.
    B. She has a gift for him.   D. His sister is napping.

22. How does Max know his parents have not forgotten his birthday?

_____

_____

23. Which word best completes the sentence?
    You should get out of the water if there is a storm _____ lightning is dangerous.
    A. although   B. because   C. if   D. so

24. Rewrite the sentence so that it is correct.
    Joanie and me are writing a report about new york city.

_____

_____

 25. Read the draft report about tigers. Then rewrite the paragraph to correct the errors you find.

> Tigers are pretty animals, but they are also very powerfull. They are the largest cats in the world, and can grow to be over ten Feet long. Tigers live in many parts of asia, but there are not that many left. They're are less than sixty South China tigers left in the world, and none of them live in the wild. That makes them the most endangeredest tigers of all.

What changes would make this paragraph better? Rewrite the report to make it better.

_____

_____

 **Answer Key**

Note: The answers to open-ended, constructed response questions are sample answers. Answers will vary, but look for the main ideas to be included.

Highlight any questions that your child gets wrong. Looking at the wrong answers may help to reveal one or more standards with which your child is struggling. Even if your child has done well on this posttest, reviewing the lessons will help him or her become a better reader and writer.

Passage	Question	Answer	Standard(s)
Untitled	1	C	RL.3.3
	2	Bella frowns.	RL.3.1
	3	D	RL.3.3
	4	C	RL.3.4
	5	B	RL.3.2
	6	She wants to decorate and play with her new playhouse.	RL.3.2, RL.3.3
The First Flight	7	Fly	RI.3.4
	8	(1) The Wright brothers open a bicycle shop. (2) The Wright brothers experiment with propellers. (3) The Wright brothers test gliders. (4) The Wright brothers fly a plane.	RI.3.3
	9	Orville and Wilbur Wright tried hard. They used what they knew about bicycles to figure out planes. They spent many years experimenting with different kinds of wings and propellers. They also tested gliders. The brothers finally figured out what would work. In 1903, they succeeded in getting the first plane off the ground.	RI.3.2, RI.3.3, W.3.2
Going Green	10	C	RI.3.1, RI.3.4
	11	B	RI.3.2
	12	A	RI.3.4
	13	A	RI.3.4
	14	The author wants people to be less wasteful. The author explains three main ways to do this. People can reduce the amount of water, electricity and other natural resources. They can reuse the things that they have instead of throwing them away. People can also recycle things.	RI.3.2, W.3.2

Passage	Question	Answer	Standard(s)
The Treasure in the Field	15	A	RL.3.3
	16	The story starts by saying that the farmer worked hard in his field to grow crops.	RL.3.1
	17	The farmer's son is lazy, because he does not want to work in the field. He tries to get money in other ways. He is also foolish, because the farmer is able to trick him into working the field.	RL.3.3, RL.3.1
	18	The farmer tells his son that there is treasure buried in the field.	RL.3.1
	19	The last sentence of the story, which reads, "And now you know the truth: every year the field holds all the treasure we need, if only we're willing to work for it."	RL.3.2, W.3.2
Max	20	A	RL.3.3
	21	A	RL.3.1, RL.3.4
	22	Max sees that his parents have bought him the tennis racket he wanted.	RL.3.1, RL.3.3
	23	B	W.3.2.c
	24	Joanie and I are writing a report about New York City.	W.3.5
	25	Tigers are pretty animals, but they are also very <u>powerful</u>. They are the largest cats in the world, and can grow to be over ten <u>feet</u> long. Tigers live in many parts of <u>Asia</u>, but there are not that many left. <u>There</u> are less than sixty South China tigers left in the world, and none of them live in the wild. That makes them the most <u>endangered</u> tigers of all.	W.3.5

MATHEMATICS POST-TEST

1. Which fraction is equal to 1?

   A. $\dfrac{1}{4}$ B. $\dfrac{2}{2}$ C. $\dfrac{2}{4}$ D. $\dfrac{4}{2}$

2. Four friends want to split a pizza. If each person brings $3, how much can they spend on the pizza? Draw an array to show your work and then write an equation to solve the problem.

   _____

   _____

3. Geneva ate $\dfrac{3}{6}$ of her sandwich. Robbie ate $\dfrac{3}{8}$ of his sandwich. If the sandwiches are the same size, who ate more? Explain how you know.

   _____

   _____

4. Which of the following can be answered by finding 6 × 3?

   A. A room has 3 rows of desks and each row has 6 desks. How many desks are in the room?

   B. A teacher started the day with 6 pencils. She gave 3 pencils to students. How many pencils does she have left?

   C. Danny's grandma gave each of her 3 grandchildren an equal share of $6. How much money did each grandchild receive?

   D. Earlier in the day, Chelsea found 6 buttons. Later, she found 3 more. How many total buttons did she find?

5. Frankie brought candy for all the members in his chess club. He gave each member 4 pieces of candy and the club sponsor 3 pieces of candy. If there are 8 members in the club, then how many pieces of candy did he give away?

   _____

   _____

6. Nadia is making mini-muffins for her teachers. If she makes 3 muffins for each of her 6 teachers, which number sentence could be used to find the total number of mini-muffins Nadia needs to bake?

   A. 6 ÷ ? = 3   B. 6 ÷ 3 = ?   C. 3 × 6 = ?   D. 3 × ? = 6

7. What is the area of the figure below?

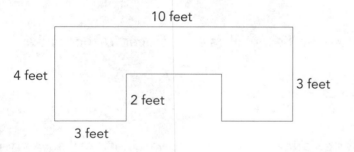

8. What number in place of *m* makes the number sentence true?

   m ÷ 4 = 8

   A. 2   B. 4   C. 8   D. 32

9. Use the bar models below to compare $\frac{2}{6}$ and $\frac{2}{8}$ by writing an inequality.

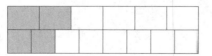

10. Erin's mom bought 15 bags of snacks. On Monday she gave 5 bags of snacks to her friends and then she gave each of her two children an equal number of snacks. How many snacks did each child get?

    A. 2   *B. 4*   *C. 5*   *D. 10*

11. A rectangle has sides of length 4 feet and 7 feet. What is the area of the rectangle?

12. Which fraction is equal to $\frac{1}{2}$?

    A. $\frac{1}{4}$ *B.* $\frac{2}{4}$ *C.* $\frac{3}{4}$ *D.* $\frac{4}{4}$

13. Write a fraction that is equivalent to $\frac{3}{4}$. Justify your answer using the model below.

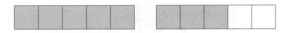

14. Express the fraction shown by the model as an improper fraction and as a mixed number.

15. Abby's parents give her an allowance of $5 per week. If Abby saves her whole allowance every week for 6 weeks, how much will she have saved? Draw a picture and write an equation to show your work.

16. Which equation represents the situation?

    "Every day Laurie practiced piano for 2 hours. How many hours did she practice in 4 days?"

    A. ◆ × 2 = 4   *B.* 4 ÷ ◆ = 2   *C.* 2 × 4 = ◆   *D.* 4 ÷ 2 = ◆

17. Anthony wants to add 35 drawings to his notebook. If he makes 5 drawings today and then 10 more tomorrow, how many drawings will he still need to make?

    A. 30   *B. 25*   *C. 20*   *D. 15*

18. What is the area of the shaded region below? Each square represents one square foot.

A. 36 square feet   C. 12 square feet
B. 9 square feet   D. 24 square feet

19. A vet gave each of the 8 cats she saw today 3 treats. Which model shows how many treats the vet gave to cats today?

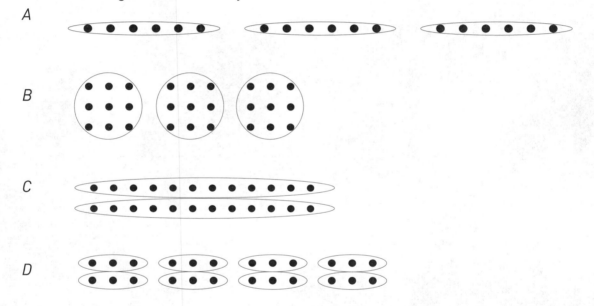

A

B

C

D

20. Stevie is mailing a box. The mail company has a rule that small boxes must be less than 14 kilograms, but Stevie's box weighs 20 kilograms. If he takes out a board game that weighs 2,000 grams and a dictionary that weighs 3 kilograms, can he mail the box?

21. ABOUT how much liquid does an average bathtub hold?
    A. 20 milliliters   B. 200 militates   C. 20 liters   D. 200 liters

22. Which expression shows the total number of smiley faces in the picture below?

☺ ☺ ☺   A.   6 + 3
☺ ☺ ☺   B.   6 × 3
☺ ☺ ☺   C.   6 − 3
☺ ☺ ☺   D.   6 ÷ 3
☺ ☺ ☺
☺ ☺ ☺

23. Which expression represents the area of the figure below?

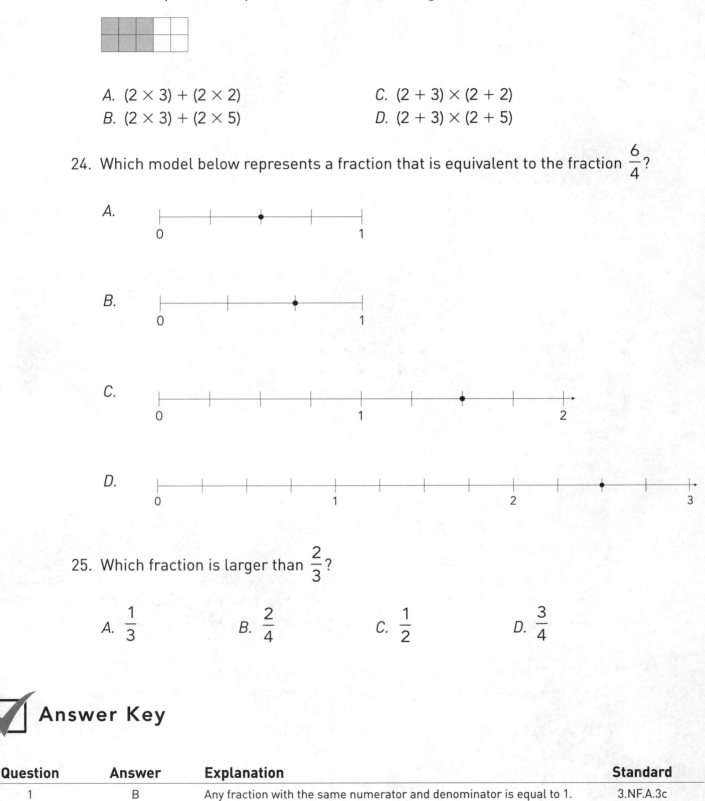

A. (2 × 3) + (2 × 2)

B. (2 × 3) + (2 × 5)

C. (2 + 3) × (2 + 2)

D. (2 + 3) × (2 + 5)

24. Which model below represents a fraction that is equivalent to the fraction $\frac{6}{4}$?

A.

B.

C.

D.

25. Which fraction is larger than $\frac{2}{3}$?

A. $\frac{1}{3}$

B. $\frac{2}{4}$

C. $\frac{1}{2}$

D. $\frac{3}{4}$

✓ Answer Key

Question	Answer	Explanation	Standard
1	B	Any fraction with the same numerator and denominator is equal to 1.	3.NF.A.3c

Question	Answer	Explanation	Standard
2	$12	$4 \times 3 = 12$	3.OA.A.3
3	Geneva	The fractions have the same numerator, so both Geneva and Robbie ate the same number of parts. The fraction with the smaller denominator has the larger parts. This means Geneva's 3 part were larger than Robbie's 3 parts, so Geneva ate more.	3.NF.A.3d
4	A	The description for part A can be thought of as an array of desks. Therefore, the total would be found using multiplication.	3.OA.A.1
5	35	$4 \times 8 + 3 = 35$	3.OA.D.8
6	C	3 (muffins) $\times$ 6 (teachers) = 18 (muffins total)	3.OA.A.4
7	32 square feet	The left and right "legs" each have an area of $4 \times 3 = 12$ square feet. The middle portion has an area of $4 \times 2 = 8$ square feet. This gives a total of $12 + 12 + 8 = 32$ square feet.	3.MD.C.7d
8	D	$32 \div 4 = 8$	3.OA.A.4
9	$\frac{2}{6} > \frac{2}{8}$	The bar models show that it takes more eighths to make a whole than it takes sixths to make a whole, so each eighth is smaller than each sixth. Thus, $\frac{2}{6}$ is greater than $\frac{2}{8}$.	3.NF.A.3d
10	C	After giving away the 5 bags, there were 10 left and $10 \div 2 = 5$.	3.OA.D.8
11	28 square feet	$4 \times 7 = 28$	3.MD.C.7b
12	B	This relation can best be seen using an area model.	3.NF.A.3a, 3.NF.A.3b
13	Sample answer: 6/8.		3.NF.A.3a, 3.NF.A.3b
14	$\frac{8}{5}, 1\frac{3}{5}$	There are 5 parts in each bar. The first bar is shaded completely, which represents $\frac{5}{5}$, or 1. The second bar has 3 of 5 parts shaded, which represents $\frac{3}{5}$.	3.NF.A.3c
15	$30	$5 \times 6 = 30$	3.OA.A.3
16	C	Since it is asking for a total given 4 groups of 2 (4 days, 2 hours each), multiplication is needed.	3.OA.A.1
17	C	$35 - 5 - 10 = 20$	3.OA.D.8

Question	Answer	Explanation	Standard
18	C	There are 12 squares shaded.	3.MD.C.7a
19	D	Because each cat was given 3 treats, the correct model should 8 sets of 3.	3.OA.A.1, 3.OA.A.3
20	No	Stevie needs to remove $20 - 14 = 6$ kilograms. The board game has a mass of 2,000 grams, which is equal to 2 kilograms. The dictionary has a mass of 3 kilograms, so Stevie removes $2 + 3 = 5$ kilograms and $5 < 6$, so the box still has too much mass to mail.	3.MD.A.2
21	D	An average bathtub holds about 200 liters of water. For reference, 20 milliliters is about 4 spoonfuls, 200 milliliters is about a child's cup, and 20 liters is about a kitchen sink.	3.MD.A.2
22	B	The total number of items in an array can always be found using multiplication.	3.OA.A.1
23	A	The area of the shaded region is 2×3 and the area of the remainder is 2×2. Together this gives the area of the entire figure.	3.MD.C.7c
24	C	$\dfrac{6}{4} = 1\dfrac{2}{4}$	3.NF.A.3a, 3.NF.A.3b
25	D	Plotting each fraction on a number line, only ¾ is to the right of 2/3.	3.NF.A.3d

Reading: Informational Text

Key Ideas and Details

1. Ask and answer questions to demonstrate understanding of a text, referring explicitly to the text as the basis for the answers.

2. Determine the main idea of a text; recount the key details and explain how they support the main idea.

3. Describe the relationship between a series of historical events, scientific ideas or concepts, or steps in technical procedures in a text, using language that pertains to time, sequence, and cause/effect.

Craft and Structure

4. Determine the meaning of general academic and domain-specific words and phrases in a text relevant to a grade 3 topic or subject area.

5. Use text features and search tools (e.g., key words, sidebars, hyperlinks) to locate information relevant to a given topic efficiently.

6. Distinguish their own point of view from that of the author of a text.

Integration of Knowledge and Ideas

7. Use information gained from illustrations (e.g., maps, photographs) and the words in a text to demonstrate understanding of the text (e.g., where, when, why, and how key events occur).

8. Describe the logical connection between particular sentences and paragraphs in a text (e.g., comparison, cause/effect, first/second/third in a sequence).

9. Compare and contrast the most important points and key details presented in two texts on the same topic.

Range of Reading and Level of Text Complexity

10. By the end of the year, read and comprehend informational texts, including history/social studies, science, and technical texts, at the high end of the grades 2-3 text complexity band independently and proficiently.

Reading: Literature

Key Ideas and Details

1. Ask and answer questions to demonstrate understanding of a text, referring explicitly to the text as the basis for the answers.

2. Recount stories, including fables, folktales, and myths from diverse cultures; determine the central message, lesson, or moral and explain how it is conveyed through key details in the text.

3. Describe characters in a story (e.g., their traits, motivations, or feelings) and explain how their actions contribute to the sequence of events

Craft and Structure

4. Determine the meaning of words and phrases as they are used in a text, distinguishing literal from nonliteral language.

5. Refer to parts of stories, dramas, and poems when writing or speaking about a text, using terms such as chapter, scene, and stanza; describe how each successive part builds on earlier sections.

6. Distinguish their own point of view from that of the narrator or those of the characters.

Integration of Knowledge and Ideas

7. Explain how specific aspects of a text's illustrations contribute to what is conveyed by the words in a story (e.g., create mood, emphasize aspects of a character or setting)

9. Compare and contrast the themes, settings, and plots of stories written by the same author about the same or similar characters (e.g., in books from a series).

Range of Reading and Level of Text Complexity

10. By the end of the year, read and comprehend literature, including stories, dramas, and poetry, at the high end of the grades 2-3 text complexity band independently and proficiently.

Reading: Foundational Skills

Phonics and Word Recognition

1. Know and apply grade-level phonics and word analysis skills in decoding words.

   a. Identify and know the meaning of the most common prefixes and derivational suffixes.
   b. Decode words with common Latin suffixes.
   c. Decode multisyllable words.
   d. Read grade-appropriate irregularly spelled words.

Fluency

2. Read with sufficient accuracy and fluency to support comprehension.

   a. Read grade-level text with purpose and understanding.
   b. Read grade-level prose and poetry orally with accuracy, appropriate rate, and expression on successive readings.
   c. Use context to confirm or self-correct word recognition and understanding, rereading as necessary.

Writing

Text Types and Purposes

1. Write opinion pieces on topics or texts, supporting a point of view with reasons.

   a. Introduce the topic or text they are writing about, state an opinion, and create an organizational structure that lists reasons.
   b. Provide reasons that support the opinion.
   c. Use linking words and phrases (e.g., *because, therefore, since, for example*) to connect opinion and reasons.
   d. Provide a concluding statement or section.

2. Write informative/explanatory texts to examine a topic and convey ideas and information clearly.

   a. Introduce a topic and group related information together; include illustrations when useful to aiding comprehension.
   b. Develop the topic with facts, definitions, and details.
   c. Use linking words and phrases (e.g., *also, another, and, more, but*) to connect ideas within categories of information.
   d. Provide a concluding statement or section.

3. Write narratives to develop real or imagined experiences or events using effective technique, descriptive details, and clear event sequences.

   a. Establish a situation and introduce a narrator and/or characters; organize an event sequence that unfolds naturally.

b. Use dialogue and descriptions of actions, thoughts, and feelings to develop experiences and events or show the response of characters to situations.

c. Use temporal words and phrases to signal event order.

d. Provide a sense of closure.

Production and Distribution of Writing

4. With guidance and support from adults, produce writing in which the development and organization are appropriate to task and purpose. (Grade-specific expectations for writing types are defined in standards 1-3 above.)

5. With guidance and support from peers and adults, develop and strengthen writing as needed by planning, revising, and editing. (Editing for conventions should demonstrate command of Language standards 1-3 up to and including grade 3 here.)

6. With guidance and support from adults, use technology to produce and publish writing (using keyboarding skills) as well as to interact and collaborate with others.

Research to Build and Present Knowledge

7. Conduct short research projects that build knowledge about a topic.

8. Recall information from experiences or gather information from print and digital sources; take brief notes on sources and sort evidence into provided categories.

Range of Writing

10. Write routinely over extended time frames (time for research, reflection, and revision) and shorter time frames (a single sitting or a day or two) for a range of discipline-specific tasks, purposes, and audiences. (Begins in Grade 4.)

Speaking & Listening

Comprehension and Collaboration

1. Engage effectively in a range of collaborative discussions (one-on-one, in groups, and teacher-led) with diverse partners on *grade 3 topics and texts*, building on others' ideas and expressing their own clearly.

a. Come to discussions prepared, having read or studied required material; explicitly draw on that preparation and other information known about the topic to explore ideas under discussion.

b. Follow agreed-upon rules for discussions (e.g., gaining the floor in respectful ways, listening to others with care, speaking one at a time about the topics and texts under discussion).

c. Ask questions to check understanding of information presented, stay on topic, and link their comments to the remarks of others.

d. Explain their own ideas and understanding in light of the discussion.

2. Determine the main ideas and supporting details of a text read aloud or information presented in diverse media and formats, including visually, quantitatively, and orally.

3. Ask and answer questions about information from a speaker, offering appropriate elaboration and detail.

Presentation of Knowledge and Ideas

4. Report on a topic or text, tell a story, or recount an experience with appropriate facts and relevant, descriptive details, speaking clearly at an understandable pace.

5. Create engaging audio recordings of stories or poems that demonstrate fluid reading at an understandable pace; add visual displays when appropriate to emphasize or enhance certain facts or details.

6. Speak in complete sentences when appropriate to task and situation in order to provide requested detail or clarification. (See grade 3 Language standards 1 and 3 here for specific expectations.)

Language

Conventions of Standard English

1. Demonstrate command of the conventions of standard English grammar and usage when writing or speaking.
   a. Explain the function of nouns, pronouns, verbs, adjectives, and adverbs in general and their functions in particular sentences.
   b. Form and use regular and irregular plural nouns.
   c. Use abstract nouns (e.g., *childhood*).
   d. Form and use regular and irregular verbs.
   e. Form and use the simple (e.g., *I walked; I walk; I will walk*) verb tenses.
   f. Ensure subject-verb and pronoun-antecedent agreement.
   g. Form and use comparative and superlative adjectives and adverbs, and choose between them depending on what is to be modified.
   h. Use coordinating and subordinating conjunctions.
   i. Produce simple, compound and complex sentences.

2. Demonstrate command of the conventions of standard English capitalization, punctuation, and spelling when writing.
   a. Capitalize appropriate words in titles.
   b. Use commas in addresses.
   c. Use commas and quotation marks in dialogue.
   d. Form and use possessives.

e. Use conventional spelling for high-frequency and other studied words and for adding suffixes to base words (e.g., *sitting, smiled, cries, happiness*).

f. Use spelling patterns and generalizations (e.g., *word families, position-based spellings, syllable patterns, ending rules, meaningful word parts*) in writing words.

g. Consult reference materials, including beginning dictionaries, as needed to check and correct spellings.

Knowledge of Language

3. Use knowledge of language and its conventions when writing, speaking, reading, or listening.

a. Choose words and phrases for effect.

b. Recognize and observe differences between the conventions of spoken and written standard English.

Vocabulary Acquisition and Use

4. Determine or clarify the meaning of unknown and multiple-meaning word and phrases based on *grade 3 reading and content*, choosing flexibly from a range of strategies.

a. Use sentence-level context as a clue to the meaning of a word or phrase.

b. Determine the meaning of the new word formed when a known affix is added to a known word (e.g., *agreeable/disagreeable, comfortable/uncomfortable, care/careless, heat/preheat*).

c. Use a known root word as a clue to the meaning of an unknown word with the same root (e.g., *company, companion*).

d. Use glossaries or beginning dictionaries, both print and digital, to determine or clarify the precise meaning of key words and phrases.

5. Demonstrate understanding of figurative language, word relationships and nuances in word meanings.

a. Distinguish the literal and nonliteral meanings of words and phrases in context (e.g., *take steps*).

b. Identify real-life connections between words and their use (e.g., describe people who are *friendly* or *helpful*).

c. Distinguish shades of meaning among related words that describe states of mind or degrees of certainty (e.g., *knew, believed, suspected, heard, wondered*).

6. Acquire and use accurately grade-appropriate conversational, general academic, and domain-specific words and phrases, including those that signal spatial and temporal relationships (e.g., *After dinner that night we went looking for them*).

Operations and Algebraic Thinking 3.OA

Represent and solve problems involving multiplication and division.

1. Interpret products of whole numbers, e.g., interpret 5×7 as the total number of objects in 5 groups of 7 objects each. *For example, describe a context in which a total number of objects can be expressed as 5×7.*

2. Interpret whole-number quotients of whole numbers, e.g., interpret $56 \div 8$ as the number of objects in each share when 56 objects are partitioned equally into 8 shares, or as a number of shares when 56 objects are partitioned into equal shares of 8 objects each. *For example, describe a context in which a number of shares or a number of groups can be expressed as $56 \div 8$.*

3. Use multiplication and division within 100 to solve word problems in situations involving equal groups, arrays, and measurement quantities, e.g., by using drawings and equations with a symbol for the unknown number to represent the problem.

4. Determine the unknown whole number in a multiplication or division equation relating three whole numbers. *For example, determine the unknown number that makes the equation true in each of the equations $8 \times ? = 48$, $5 = \square \div 3$, $6 \times 6 = ?$.*

Understand properties of multiplication and the relationship between multiplication and division.

5. Apply properties of operations as strategies to multiply and divide.2 *Examples: If $6 \times 4 = 24$ is known, then $4 \times 6 = 24$ is also known. (Commutative property of multiplication.) $3 \times 5 \times 2$ can be found by $3 \times 5 = 15$ then $15 \times 2 = 30$, or by $5 \times 2 = 10$, then $3 \times 10 = 30$. (Associative property of multiplication.) Knowing that $8 \times 5 = 40$ and $8 \times 2 = 16$, one can find 8×7 as $8 \times (5 + 2) = (8 \times 5) + (8 \times 2) = 40 + 16 = 56$. (Distributive property.)*

6. Understand division as an unknown-factor problem. *For example, find $32 \div 8$ by finding the number that makes 32 when multiplied by 8.*

Multiply and divide within 100.

7. Fluently multiply and divide within 100, using strategies such as the relationship between

multiplication and division (e.g., knowing that $8 \times 5 = 40$, one knows $40 \div 5 = 8$) or properties of operations. By the end of Grade 3, know from memory all products of two one-digit numbers.

Solve problems involving the four operations, and identify and explain patterns in arithmetic.

8. Solve two-step word problems using the four operations. Represent these problems using equations with a letter standing for the unknown quantity. Assess the reasonableness of answers using mental computation and estimation strategies including rounding.3

9. Identify arithmetic patterns (including patterns in the addition table or multiplication table), and explain them using properties of operations. *For example, observe that 4 times a number is always even, and explain why 4 times a number can be decomposed into two equal addends.*

Number and Operations in Base Ten 3.NBT

Use place value understanding and properties of operations to perform multi-digit arithmetic.4

1. Use place value understanding to round whole numbers to the nearest 10 or 100.

2. Fluently add and subtract within 1000 using strategies and algorithms based on place value, properties of operations, and/or the relationship between addition and subtraction.

3. Multiply one-digit whole numbers by multiples of 10 in the range 10–90 (e.g., 9×80, 5×60) using strategies based on place value and properties of operations.

Number and Operations—Fractions5 3.NF

Develop understanding of fractions as numbers.

4. Understand a fraction $1/b$ as the quantity formed by 1 part when a whole is partitioned into b equal parts; understand a fraction a/b as the quantity formed by a parts of size $1/b$.

5. Understand a fraction as a number on the number line; represent fractions on a number line diagram.

    a. Represent a fraction $1/b$ on a number line diagram by defining the interval from 0 to 1 as the whole and partitioning it into b equal parts. Recognize that each part has size $1/b$ and that the endpoint of the part based at 0 locates the number $1/b$ on the number line.

b. Represent a fraction *a/b* on a number line diagram by marking off *a* lengths 1/*b* from 0. Recognize that the resulting interval has size *a/b* and that its endpoint locates the number *a/b* on the number line.

6. Explain equivalence of fractions in special cases, and compare fractions by reasoning about their size.

a. Understand two fractions as equivalent (equal) if they are the same size, or the same point on a number line.

b. Recognize and generate simple equivalent fractions, e.g., 1/2 = 2/4, 4/6 = 2/3. Explain why the fractions are equivalent, e.g., by using a visual fraction model.

c. Express whole numbers as fractions, and recognize fractions that are equivalent to whole numbers. *Examples: Express 3 in the form 3 = 3/1; recognize that 6/1 = 6; locate 4/4 and 1 at the same point of a number line diagram.*

d. Compare two fractions with the same numerator or the same denominator by reasoning about their size. Recognize that comparisons are valid only when the two fractions refer to the same whole. Record the results of comparisons with the symbols >, =, or <, and justify the conclusions, e.g., by using a visual fraction model.

Measurement and Data 3.MD

Solve problems involving measurement and estimation of intervals of time, liquid volumes, and masses of objects.

1. Tell and write time to the nearest minute and measure time intervals in minutes. Solve word problems involving addition and subtraction of time intervals in minutes, e.g., by representing the problem on a number line diagram. A range of algorithms may be used. Grade 3 expectations in this domain are limited to fractions with denominators 2, 3, 4, 6, and 8.

2. Measure and estimate liquid volumes and masses of objects using standard units of grams (g), kilograms (kg), and liters (l).6 Add, subtract, multiply, or divide to solve one-step word problems involving masses or volumes that are given in the same units, e.g., by using drawings (such as a beaker with a measurement scale) to represent the problem.

Represent and interpret data.

3. Draw a scaled picture graph and a scaled bar graph to represent a data set with several categories. Solve one- and two-step "how many more" and "how many less" problems using information presented in scaled bar graphs. *For example, draw a bar graph in which each square in the bar graph might represent 5 pets.*

4. Generate measurement data by measuring lengths using rulers marked with halves and fourths of an inch. Show the data by making a line plot, where the horizontal scale is marked off in appropriate units—whole numbers, halves, or quarters.

Geometric measurement: understand concepts of area and relate area to multiplication and to addition.

5. Recognize area as an attribute of plane figures and understand concepts of area measurement.

   a. A square with side length 1 unit, called "a unit square," is said to have "one square unit" of area, and can be used to measure area.

   b. A plane figure which can be covered without gaps or overlaps by n unit squares is said to have an area of n square units.

6. Measure areas by counting unit squares (square cm, square m, square in, square ft, and improvised units).

7. Relate area to the operations of multiplication and addition.

   a. Find the area of a rectangle with whole-number side lengths by tiling it, and show that the area is the same as would be found by multiplying the side lengths.

   b. Multiply side lengths to find areas of rectangles with whole number side lengths in the context of solving real world and mathematical problems, and represent whole-number products as rectangular areas in mathematical reasoning.

   c. Use tiling to show in a concrete case that the area of a rectangle with whole-number side lengths a and $b + c$ is the sum of $a \times b$ and $a \times c$. Use area models to represent the distributive property in mathematical reasoning.

   d. Recognize area as additive. Find areas of rectilinear figures by decomposing them into non-overlapping rectangles and adding the areas of the non-overlapping parts, applying this technique to solve real world problems.

Geometric measurement: recognize perimeter as an attribute of plane figures and distinguish between linear and area measures.

8. Solve real world and mathematical problems involving perimeters of polygons, including finding the perimeter given the side lengths, finding an unknown side length, and exhibiting rectangles with the same perimeter and different areas or with the same area and different perimeters.

Geometry 3.G

Reason with shapes and their attributes.

1. Understand that shapes in different categories (e.g., rhombuses, rectangles, and others) may share attributes (e.g., having four sides), and that the shared attributes can define a larger category (e.g., quadrilaterals). Recognize rhombuses, rectangles, and squares as examples of quadrilaterals, and draw examples of quadrilaterals that do not belong to any of these subcategories.

2. Partition shapes into parts with equal areas. Express the area of each part as a unit fraction of the whole. *For example, partition a shape into 4 parts with equal area, and describe the area of each part as 1/4 of the area of the shape.*